*"It is a lovely thing to live
with courage, and die leaving
an everlasting fame."*

—Alexander

Previous spreads:

A helmeted Alexander the Great prepares to spear a lion in this fourth-century BC pebble mosaic unearthed at Pella, the capital of ancient Macedon. The second hunter, at right, may be Alexander's lifelong companion, Hephaestion.

French artist Charles Le Brun captures the Battle of the Granicus in this seventeenth-century oil painting, in which Alexander, wearing a distinctive plumed helmet, is the central figure. The historic confrontation with Persian imperial forces at the Granicus River in Asia Minor was the crucial first pitched battle in the young king's Asian campaign.

A scene from the Alexander Sarcophagus shows Greeks and Persians in battle. The fourth-century BC sarcophagus was discovered at Sidon, Lebanon, in 1887. The marble coffin's occupant is unknown, but it was not Alexander. The sarcophagus bears his name because his exploits are the theme of the friezes that cover its sides.

Copyright details appear on page 210.

ALEXANDER
THE CONQUEROR
The Epic Story of the Warrior King

DA CAPO PRESS
A Member of the Perseus Books Group

A TEHABI BOOK

CONTENTS

FOREWORD

"What? Alexander dead? Impossible! The world would reek of his corpse!" So exclaimed a local orator when news of the Macedonian king's death reached Athens in the summer of 323 BC. To many, such a characterization was warranted. Yet in a speech given in 1980 at a major museum display of Macedonian antiquities, the president of the Hellenic Republic proclaimed, "As for Greece, Alexander has served as no other man has done the dreams of the nation, as a symbol of indissoluble unity and continuity between ancient and modern Hellenism."

A monumental stinking corpse. A heroic national icon. Nearly twenty-three centuries separate the distinctly opposite views of these two Greeks. Alexander, king of Macedonians, whose spectacular career of conquest made him arguably the most famous secular leader in history, remains an enduring and controversial figure in European and western Asian history, folklore, and art. From the Atlantic to India, there is hardly a people who have not incorporated into their public consciousness some aspect—real or imagined, friendly or hostile—of Alexander's exploits. The diversity of opinion represented by both that ancient Athenian orator and the modern Greek politician continues unabated into our own age.

Opposite: The Greeks and Persians engage in battle in the Alexander Sarcophagus, whose reliefs are esteemed as among the finest carvings in the ancient world.

Previous spread: This pebble mosaic from the Roman era shows Alexander, javelin poised, bearing down on the chariot of the Persian king Darius at the Battle of Issus. The mosaic, found in a villa at Pompeii, copies a Hellenistic painting of the historic battle, done a generation after Alexander's death. Thus the scene is the most contemporary rendering of the battle to survive today.

Alexander ranks among the greatest military commanders of all time. King at the age of twenty, conqueror of the Persian Empire at twenty-five, explorer of the boundaries of the known world at thirty, and dead before he reached his thirty-third birthday—his was a stunning career and the stuff of legends. Roman generals competed with his legend, and later, Roman emperors imitated him. He became a central figure in medieval European romantic literature and in the written and oral traditions of peoples from the British Isles to southeast Asia. And in present-day Greece, the Macedonian Alexander, ruler of the ancient Greek cities, has even been resurrected as a national hero, the symbol linking the modern nation to a famous distant past. There is no one else anywhere quite like him.

In modern times, his legend has evolved as a metaphor for fame. A *New York Times* book reviewer once described Albert Einstein as "the Alexander the Great of the life of the mind." When, in *Hamlet*, Shakespeare sought a historical figure to contrast the immortality of fame with the perishable nature of the human body, he chose Alexander. And when Donald Trump developed the elaborate suites on the fifty-first floor of his Taj Mahal casino-hotel in Atlantic City, he named the most extravagant of his suites after the Macedonian conqueror.

There is no doubt about the continuing extraordinary fame of Alexander of Macedon. His legend is part of a very long popular tradition, and one that is permanently fixed in the public consciousness. Yet to serious students of history, this sensational portrait of Alexander is incomplete. And so they continue to unearth more details of his life. The central problem in understanding Alexander is that there is little evidence surviving directly from his own time. The earliest extant narrative account of his life was written nearly three centuries after his death, and our best history postdates the king's career by about five centuries. Fragments of the original (and now lost) sources are mentioned in the surviving accounts, but some of these passed through several hands before assuming the corrupted form in which we now have them. Briefly put, we have very poor evidence documenting the life of one of the most famous individuals in history.

The enduring task of scholars is to validate the information that has come down to us. And yet, while the general outlines of Alexander's march through Asia are clear, we are more often than not left to speculate about nuances: his plans, the details of some battles, the Macedonian logistical and intelligence operations, and his relationships with the members of his own entourage as well as the foreigners he encountered.

Laura Foreman understands the difficulty of working with such problematic evidence and has applied a necessary and judicious restraint in developing her portrait of the king. As a consultant, I took pleasure in working with her and in watching her portrait of Alexander emerge. Although I made a number of suggestions about details, I did not attempt to interfere with her vision of the king. The reader may feel confident that Laura Foreman's portrait of Alexander is based on both a rational assessment of the evidence and, for nuances, her sensitivity to the complexity of human nature.

Eugene N. Borza
Professor Emeritus of Ancient History
The Pennsylvania State University

CHAPTER ONE

[AGE 0–20   YEAR 356–336 BC]

THE PRINCE

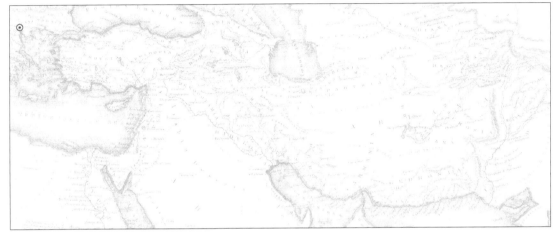

Above: A third-century BC head of the young Alexander by an unknown sculptor exemplifies the tousled hair and idealized features typical of the prince's portraiture. In life, Alexander allowed only one artist, Lysippos, to sculpt him, and today no detailed likeness done from life survives.

Above: Philip of Macedon, Alexander's father, is depicted in this ivory head dating from the fourth century BC. The piece was among statuary unearthed during a late twentieth-century, Greek-led excavation of the Macedonian royal tombs at Vergina.

Opposite: Despite the lavish trappings of a Burgundian court, this fifteenth-century Flemish rendering of Alexander's birth contains some classical elements associated with his nativity. The medallion above his mother's bed, for example, bears the image of a dragon, alluding to ancient legends that Alexander was sired by a god in the shape of a dragon or snake.

THERE WAS A TIME when earth and heaven were not so separate as they are now. Gods dabbled freely in human affairs, directing mortals toward good or ill, blessing or cursing them, even siring or bearing their children. And a select few mortals, if the gods favored them and their deeds were great enough, might aspire to divinity themselves—or so most people believed. Signs and portents often heralded the advent of these special children of destiny, and thus it was with Alexander of Macedon.

It was said, for instance, that on the night Alexander was born in the summer of 356 BC, the magnificent temple of Artemis at Ephesus burned because the goddess was away attending the labor of his royal mother. The fire, some prophesied, meant that the child would one day rage like a conflagration

through Asia Minor and beyond. And even before the birth there were omens. A few months after his marriage to Olympias, a princess of Epirus, King Philip II of Macedon had a dream in which he was closing his wife's vagina with a seal whose wax bore the image of a lion's head. This meant Olympias was pregnant, a palace seer assured the king. The child would be a son, lionlike and strong in spirit. Olympias also had a vision and, characteristically, hers was more wildly dramatic. The night before her wedding, she said, a bolt of lightning had torn into her, igniting a fire that gushed from her womb and flamed far along the earth before it was quenched. Surely this signaled an exalted fate (not to say a miraculous celestial parentage) for the boy she would bear.

Even with such auguries, it is doubtful that Philip and Olympias could have envisioned just how unique their child would be, that he would accomplish things no man had ever done. On the other hand, perhaps they did know Alexander's potential. They were people who imagined and strove for a great deal, and they lived in a time of constant upheaval and, therefore, constant possibilities.

◆　◆　◆

Greece, in their day, was not a nation. It was a collection of city-states—nearly a thousand of them, large and small—that dotted the Greek peninsula, the islands of the Aegean Sea, and eastward across the sea, the coast of Asia Minor (modern Turkey). These were independent, self-governing entities, wary of encroachment, and in one combination or another they were almost always at war. They fought for land or resources or pride or honor or glory, or simply because it was their way of life. They could make common cause, however, if it was in their interest, and particularly if they faced a common threat.

They had faced such a threat about a century and a half before Philip's time. It loomed in the form of a huge and wealthy Persian Empire intent on expanding to the west, and most of the city-states did unite to throw back the invaders. The Persian Wars produced heroes who were legends in Greece, among them the three hundred Spartans who for three days held the pass at Thermopylae, the gateway to central Greece, against a Persian army numbering in the hundreds of thousands. Against all odds, the Greeks eventually defeated the Persians on sea and land, thanks largely to Athenian maritime strength and Spartan military

Above: A heroic statue of the Spartan king Leonidas stands at Thermopylae, where the three hundred Spartans he led stood their ground against hordes of invading Persians in the Greco–Persian wars of the early fifth century BC. The Spartans died to the last man.

Opposite: A map of the Aegean world at the time of Alexander's birth includes Macedon, Greece, and the western part of Asia Minor. Ancient Macedon was made up of portions of modern Greece, Bulgaria, and the Republic of Macedonia.

Below: This small, bronze sculpture of a Spartan cavalryman and his mount dates from the sixth century BC and is among the earliest artworks to survive from western Greece. The Spartans' bravery was always legendary, but their clumsy efforts to force their harsh, martial lifestyle on their neighbors helped lead to their downfall.

prowess on land. But this was no sooner done than the usual feuds and rivalries resurfaced, and within a few decades the two most powerful city-states, Athens and Sparta, were embroiled in the worst internal conflict of all, the Peloponnesian War.

The combatants bled each other for nearly thirty years before Sparta finally won the war—and utterly lost the peace. Through brutality, inflexibility, and simple stupidity, the Spartans managed to alienate almost all of their neighbors and allies. After their defeat at the hands of Thebes in 371 BC, they shrank sullenly back into the Peloponnese to continue their slow decline. Thebes was now on the ascendant militarily, but it remained unclear whether she, or any state, would succeed Athens or Sparta as the preeminent power in Greece.

◆ ◆ ◆

That Macedon might rise to fill this void would have seemed at the time the most improbable of long shots; this loosely basted quilt of highland and lowland kingships lying along Greece's northern border had never figured more than marginally in the momentous affairs to the south. To begin with, Macedonians were not even Greek. They were ethnically distinct, largely because they did not share the Bronze Age antecedent, the Mycenaean civilization that helped define what it meant to be Greek. The Macedonians had their own language (though Greek was the tongue of the elite and the royal court) and certain customs and traditions of their own.

Geographically, Macedon had potential. Its plains, guarded by a semicircle of mountains to the north, west, and south, were watered by four rivers and were wondrously fertile, rich in both crops and cattle. On the east there was easy access to the Thermaic Gulf, a northern arm of the Aegean. There were minerals, including gold and silver, and the mountains bristled with timber that was excellent for shipbuilding.

Politically, however, Macedon was hardly a recognizable unit in the time before Philip. In the centuries from its first appearance in history, Lower Macedon—the lowlands—had been ruled by a single dynasty, the Argeads. The mountainous region, Upper Macedon, was divided into three tribal lands whose chieftans deemed themselves kings in their own right. Over the years, the lowlanders had become Hellenized to some degree, while the highlanders often had more in common with the tribal societies on their outer borders than they did with the Argead court or the Macedonians of the plain. Keeping Upper Macedon in the fold was an ongoing concern for the Argead kings.

Above: This fourth-century relief found in the Athenian harbor town of Piraeus was sacred to the Thracian goddess Bendis. Her cult was imported into Athens around 432 BC at the outbreak of the Peloponnesian War.

Left: An Athenian warrior preparing for battle ties on his greaves, or shin armor, in this scene on a sixth-century BC Attic black-figure vase. Black-figure pottery flourished in Athens for more than 250 years until the fifth century BC.

Opposite: The work of Macedonian artisans, this beautiful mosaic floor survives in the ruins of the royal palace at Pella. In Alexander's day, the king's residence actually consisted of two buildings.

So was proving themselves to the Greek world. All Macedonian dynasts, lowland and highland, claimed Greek descent, an assertion that may or may not have reflected their true origins but certainly revealed their attitude: To be Greek was an enviable, superior thing. Greece, particularly Athens, was the heart of the civilized world, and if Macedon were ever to be more than a despised backwater, it must somehow become more Greek. Several Argeads strove hard toward this end, among them one Archelaus who, in the fifth century BC, moved from the ancient capital of Aegae and reestablished his court a few miles to the northeast at Pella. Among other things, Pella offered easier access to the Thermaic Gulf and therefore to southern Greece. Archelaus established a festival for arts and athletics in imitation of the Olympic Games—restricted to Greeks at that time—and he imported a famous Athenian painter and Athenian artisans to adorn his new palace. Setting himself up as a patron of the arts, he tried to lure famous names from Athens, and with some success. Most notably, the great Euripides, though by then in his eighties, moved to Macedon and wrote his last and perhaps his most brilliant play, the *Bacchae*.

Above: This marble bust of the playwright Euripides is a copy of a fourth-century Greek original. Along with their beauty of language, Euripides' tragedies are remarkable for their profound insights into the human psyche, particularly the thoughts and emotions of women.

Left: Philip's toughness and shrewdness are well captured in this portrait, a copy of a fourth-century Greek original.

Previous spread: The Athenian acropolis is crowned by the ruins of the Parthenon, the magnificent temple of Athena, the city's patron goddess. In Greek, *parthenon* means "apartment of the virgin." Over the centuries, the building also served as a Christian church and an Islamic mosque.

But this cultural vaccination did not entirely take; in fact, it never extended far beyond the royal court. Most Macedonians much preferred their traditional rough pleasures—hunting, gambling, drinking, and philandering—to the refinements of the south. This was just as well, perhaps, because the Greeks generally regarded Macedonian aspirations with smug disdain. To them these outlanders, while not exactly barbarians (that term was usually reserved for Persians), were close enough: unmannered, uncultivated, cowardly, perfidious louts; ineffectual in war and unreliable as allies; hard drinkers and enthusiastic and indiscriminate fornicators with a special penchant for incest and sodomy. They were, in short, the hillbillies and rednecks of their day.

Moreover, while most of the city-states were oligarchies—and a few even democracies—Macedon clung to feudalism and monarchy, and not even a tidy monarchy at that. Macedonian kings were usually polygamous, and more wives tended to mean more children and thus more claimants to the throne. The eldest son might have a leg up, but primogeniture

Right: A handsome marble head of Alexander by the classical Greek sculptor Euphranor exemplifies the ancient practice of depicting royal subjects to resemble gods. Alexander was often made to look like Apollo, god of the sun and prophecy, and the ideal of male beauty.

was not a hard and fast rule, and royal succession was apt to be a confused and bloody affair. Archelaus, for instance, had murdered an uncle, cousin, and half brother on his way to the throne. He also married his father's widow, and his reign eventually ended with his assassination at the hands of a male lover. Such goings-on hardly commanded respect in the relatively orderly domains of Athens, Thebes, or Corinth.

Macedonians were well aware of the Greeks' contempt, and perhaps it helped shape their character. In the main they were a defensive, prideful, touchy lot, quick to take offense and slow to forget a slight. They chafed under their southern neighbors' scorn, but as the years passed there seemed little they could do to dispel it. Then, in 360 or 359 BC, Philip ascended to the throne, soon to display an ambition that must have at first seemed laughable: He did not merely want to impress the Greeks; he meant to rule them.

◆ ◆ ◆

In years to come, the mere suggestion that his father was a better man was enough to make Alexander the Great murder a close friend who had once saved his life. That Alexander would wholly eclipse Philip in history was beyond doubt. Yet in his lifetime, comparison to his father always touched a raw nerve in the son. It was as though no achievement, feat, or conquest was enough to hold at bay some deep fear in Alexander that he did not quite measure up.

And indeed, Philip had set a soaring standard. Barely into his twenties when he became king, he stabilized Macedon and made it the foremost state in the Hellenic world, extending his sway over almost all the Greek mainland. Before assassination abbreviated his life in 336 BC, he even stood on the verge of a campaign to invade the vast Persian Empire. Yet at the outset of this extraordinary career, odds seemed long that he would even be able to hold the Macedonian throne—or for that matter, reach it.

Philip was the third son of Amyntas III, a weak king, and a formidable highland princess named Eurydice. Amyntas was in his sixties when all three of their boys were born, predictably giving rise to rumors—unverifiable, of course—that they were bastards. Little is known of Philip's childhood except that it must have offered a broad education, and not just at the hands of his Greek tutor.

Born into the crude and rowdy Macedonian court, he must have mastered its manly pursuits early—and as an adult he would retain his taste for several of them. He would have learned to ride as soon as he could walk, and to hunt soon thereafter, most likely appreciating fine horse-flesh. As a man he would be devoted to Macedonia's strong, red wine and to the heady pleasures of sex. And he would become a renowned womanizer, with an eye, too, for the occasional handsome young man.

Philip also learned early and well the perils and prospects of being a Macedonian prince. He was in his early teens when Amyntas died and Philip's eldest brother became King Alexander II, soon to be assassinated by a certain Ptolemy, who was Eurydice's lover. Ptolemy then became regent for the next boy, Perdiccas, who was not yet of age. Witnessing the usual murderous court intrigues left Philip with few illusions about his fellow man; he would always expect people to act according to their own best interests and worst instincts, and they would seldom disappoint him. Fortunately, the boy carried into manhood a sunny disposition and genial humor that leavened his cynicism and allowed him to observe human foibles with as much amusement as contempt.

When Philip was fifteen, Ptolemy included him in a group of hostages sent to Thebes in an effort to conclude an alliance. Exchanging hostages was a customary and usually hospitable arrangement, and Philip was welcomed into the home of a fine Theban general named Pammenes, who was close friends with an even better general, the great Epaminondas. Epaminondas was the conqueror of Sparta and arguably the best military strategist Europe had thus far produced. Bringing the highly intelligent young Philip into contact with these men would prove momentous for Greece and later for Asia as well, for he would absorb their techniques, refine them, and then pass them along to his son, who would become their grand master.

Meanwhile, back in Macedon, Philip's second brother waited patiently until he had come of age, at which time he summarily murdered his mother's lover, Ptolemy, dispatched a few rivals, and in 365 BC became King Perdiccas III. He called Philip home and wisely set him to restructuring and retraining the Macedonian army. Unfortunately, the task must have been as yet incomplete by 360 or 359 BC, when Perdiccas was killed in a disastrous battle against the Illyrians, a strong and warlike tribe on Macedon's western border. Philip was thus in line to become King Philip II. He was twenty-two years old.

At first his prospects looked grim. Illyria was poised to invade from the west, and to the north another hostile tribe was encroaching on Macedonian territory. Before these threats could even be addressed, however, there was the internal matter of five other claimants to the

Above: Warriors of the tribal Illyrians, whose lands bordered Macedon, wore helmets of this type. Its characteristics included fixed cheek guards and the absence of a nosepiece.

Opposite: The Field of Cadmus near Thebes was named for the legendary founder of the city. Myth holds that Cadmus created the forebearers of the city's leading families here by sowing dragon's teeth, which sprang from the ground as fully armed noble warriors.

MAJESTY IN MACEDON

In the tradition of Argead kings, Philip was an autocrat; he was the last word in such vital matters as justice, finances, and war. Even so, there was little in his daily life to suggest such exalted status, his late-blooming aspiration to divinity notwithstanding. Like his ancestors, he was not a distant and adored monarch but more like a tribal chief among chieftains, first among equals.

He wore no crown, nor, in fact, any special insignia or regalia of any kind, aside from a small cloth filet that he donned for formal occasions. Similarly, he invoked no title. His nobles called him by his first name, and he signed his official papers merely as "Philip," not "King Philip."

He did live in a palace, but court life was highly informal, with minimal protocol and ceremony and certainly no bowing and scraping by his subject nobles. This was especially true at the symposia, the wine-soaked dinner parties for which the Macedonians were notorious. Philip's courtiers were an independent and sometimes ornery lot who felt no compunction in speaking their mind to the king, and doubtless the drunker the franker.

Such familiarity was a by-product of the very nature of Macedonian kingship: A king's power was less institutional than personal—as absolute as he was able to make it. A strong and popular king commanded great feudal loyalty; a weak one was apt to be deposed or killed by his subjects. Few, if any, Argead rulers died of old age.

Fortunately for Philip, he was strong and popular in the extreme. He was a man confident in his power, and he wore it lightly and usually with grace. Informality suited his easygoing personality.

It sat less well on Alexander. Though he was loved by the army and enjoyed the companionship of a close circle of friends, some quality always set him apart—perhaps his very greatness, perhaps some insecurity that helped fuel it. More intense than his father, lacking his humor, he was probably more vulnerable than Philip ever would have been to the lure of majesty he would encounter in the East. Persian kingship was unimaginably different from the Macedonian variety, and in trying to bridge the gulf between the two, Alexander the Great would soon encounter a battle he simply could not win. ▨

Above: Treasures unearthed from the royal Macedonian tombs at Vergina include this silver vase. A detail of its lion-skin embellishment is shown on page 58.

Right: A fourth-century Athenian red-figure goblet painted by the artist Kleophon depicts a symposium, or dinner party. Symposia were popular throughout the Greek world, but the gatherings in Macedon were widely deplored as excessively drunken and rowdy. Greeks especially frowned on the Macedonian habit of drinking wine straight, rather than mixed with water.

throne. Three were Philip's half brothers, and the remaining two had strong foreign backing. Amazingly, he managed to have all of them killed or neutralized in only a few weeks.

Killing off the opposition was typically Macedonian, of course, but the methods were purely Philip's. He could have mustered force but chose instead diplomacy to persuade others to do most of the work for him. It was a sign of things to come. Although a matchless general in his time, he would fight only as a last resort—not because he was a good-hearted fellow but because he was a pragmatist to the core: Well-trained manpower was valuable, and it was foolish to expend it when some easy words, empty promises, or ready cash would accomplish the same end. Philip hated waste.

In any case, he was just as good at negotiation as he was at war. His diplomacy was a glittering trident of shrewdness, charm, and bribery. The charm was considerable, the bribery lavish, and nobody could rival Philip at sizing up a target, off the battlefield as well as on. Thus he would proceed for more than two decades: securing his borders, bending fractious highlanders to lowland authority at home, and then looking beyond Macedon, jauntily making treaties and breaking them, playing enemies against each other, winning over adversaries, fighting when he had to. And year by year, many of Greece's city-states and its few remaining kingdoms fell into his firm, if amiable, grip.

There was, of course, resistance. The Spartans declined an alliance and Philip let them be, reasoning they were too weak to pose much of a threat. Far more worrisome was Athens, where the influential orator Demosthenes led an anti-Macedonian faction that railed ceaselessly at Philip's vaulting ambition and relentless intrusion into Greece. In fact, the more powerful city-states—and certainly lofty Athens—were no less prone to grab-it-and-growl expansionism than he was. Philip was just infinitely better at it.

Eventually, he would not be able to avoid a showdown with Athens and her allies, with the fate of Greece hanging in the balance. By the time it came, however, Philip would number among his assets the most formidable ally imaginable: his son.

◆　◆　◆

Averse as he was to fighting, Philip did choose to do battle early in his reign. Displaying all he had learned in Thebes to withering effect, he crushed the Illyrians. That done, he promptly married an Illyrian princess. He considered matrimony an unusually reliable way of assuring future loyalty and cementing alliances, and even by Macedonian standards he was an ardent polygamist.

He would marry five times (perhaps seven; sometimes two notable mistresses are included in records of his life. In those days the legal niceties were not all that important). After the Illyrian, he wed a highland Macedonian princess, and then a liaison with a Thessalian dancing girl produced a son, Arrhidaeus. But both his wives died early, the first while giving birth to a daughter. His third bride would last much longer and be of far greater consequence: She was Olympias, mother of Alexander.

Her parents were dead, but she was a princess of the ancient Molossian dynasty of Epirus and the niece and ward of the king. Epirus, which bordered Macedon on the southwest, was Greek, but like Macedon it was a monarchy and was primitive by Greek standards. And, like Macedon, Epirus seemed to produce females of extraordinary toughness and drive, if not extraordinary virtue. The women of southern Greece were generally nonentities, considered far inferior in a man's world. But their northern sisters—the royal ones, at least—sometimes injected themselves into men's affairs with tenacity and force. Certainly this would prove the case with Philip's princess bride.

Legend has it that Philip and Olympias first met when they were being initiated into a mystery cult on the northern Aegean island of Samothrace. Philip would have been in his early twenties, square-jawed and darkly handsome before innumerable battles would leave him scarred, one-eyed, and lame. Olympias would have been about ten years younger but already stunning. Supposedly they fell wildly in love. It is easy enough to imagine young passions igniting in the feverish atmosphere of torchlit, orgiastic rites, but the pretty story is probably a myth; it would be four years and two wives and a mistress later before the king would press suit. In any case, love, or the lack of it, was beside the point. The notion that romantic love and marriage are linked is quite modern, and it probably would have struck both Philip and Olympias as eccentric, not to say incomprehensible. They understood quite well that marriage was about politics and progeny; if the couple got on well, so much the better.

Above: The head of Philip appears on a Roman medallion dating from the third century AD. In this portrait he wears the headband that was the only royal insignia distinguishing Macedonian kings.

Left: Alexander's mother, Olympias, is featured in raised relief on a gold medallion, minted in the third century AD. Alexander corresponded faithfully with his mother during his long absence from home, and he was entirely devoted to her. Even so, he sometimes found her meddling a nuisance. He once joked wryly that she exacted a high rent for the nine months he spent in her womb.

Opposite: Like Macedon, Olympias's homeland of Epirus was a place of majestic highlands and fertile valleys. The rural landscape there has changed little since her day.

As to progeny, the two fell to work right away, for Alexander was born within a year of the marriage, and a daughter, Cleopatra, came a year or two later. Yet thereafter there was only drought. Some speculated that certain of his wife's more bizarre proclivities drove Philip from the connubial bed rather early. For one thing, the bed had snakes in it.

Olympias was a priestess of Dionysus and was fervent in her devotion to this strange god. Believers held that he had come from the East many years before, bringing the Greeks grapes to be cultivated for wine. Dionysus was a god of ecstasy and mystical transcendence, and his rites, which attracted many women, were mysterious and wild. Olympias was said to be adept at achieving the trancelike state of possession that supposedly figured in the rituals, and it may have been such a trance that brought on her vision of being impregnated by celestial fire. It was also said that the ceremonies sometimes involved snake handling and that Olympias maintained the creatures as pets, keeping them close to her even when she slept. Philip once saw her embracing one of the serpents, and the great oracle at Delphi told him he had witnessed his wife being visited by a god in snake form and that it would cost him an eye. He did lose the eye in battle not long thereafter.

Snakes aside, Olympias was difficult. She was quarrelsome, meddlesome, and intense, even histrionic, and imperiously insistent that all show her the respect she felt she was due. She was royal in her own right, after all, and in Alexander she possessed the one precious commodity that assured power for the wife of a polygamous king: the heir apparent. The illegitimate Arrhidaeus was lowborn on his mother's side, and some historians suggest he may also have been mentally deficient. This is probably untrue, but it is certain that he could in no way compete with his younger half brother. From the beginning, Alexander was golden in every way. He was a beautiful boy, strong, inquisitive, and enormously bright. Whatever their feelings for each other, Philip and Olympias regarded their son as a treasure, and they cooperated to maximize his potential, to groom and educate him in a way befitting the next Argead king.

◆　◆　◆

There are few stories of Alexander's early childhood, and some that exist are open to doubt. Like the omens prefiguring his birth, tales of his precocity suggest ex post facto efforts to glorify the great conqueror. Nevertheless, the precocity was doubtless a fact. Like Philip, Alexander spent his early years in a court where tough realities intruded early on childhood innocence, especially if the child was perceptive and quick. He had to grow up fast.

Below: A Greek votive sculpture depicts rites in the mystery worship of Dionysus, the god especially venerated by Olympias. The mystery religions were so called because initiates were privy to secret ceremonies forbidden to outsiders.

Previous spread: A fifth-century BC Corinthian tablet portrays a scene of ritual sacrifice to the gods. The sacrificing of oil, grain, and animals was integral to nearly all public celebrations in Greece and Macedon.

Above: A fresco from ancient Rome shows the centaur Charon teaching young Achilles to play the lyre. Alexander's interest in the instrument may have been inspired by his legendary hero's supposed proficiency with it.

Above: This terra-cotta Etruscan head of Zeus dates from the late fifth century BC. For all his majesty, the king of the Greek gods sometimes appears in myths as almost laughably human. For instance, several stories show him as a henpecked philanderer, forever trying to elude the jealous tirades of his wife and sister, Hera.

It may also be true that even as a boy he was mindful of a special destiny and was moving impatiently toward it. He was following in the footsteps of a renowned and powerful father, and from Olympias he may have had intimations of an even loftier sire. It is not known when or even whether Olympias shared with him her belief that he was fathered by a god. Regardless, Alexander was well aware of his exalted lineage on both sides. The Argeads claimed descent from Heracles, the son of Zeus by a mortal woman, the hero whose strength and courage earned him semidivine status. As for the Molossians, they traced their ancestry to Achilles, protagonist of Homer's *Iliad*, foremost of the Greek heroes in the Trojan War. The thought that this champion's blood ran in his veins must have stirred Alexander beyond all telling, for he loved the *Iliad* as a child and throughout his life. Achilles, the glorious, doomed young warrior-king, was his paradigm.

ALEXANDER AND THE ILIAD

Written nearly four hundred years before Alexander's birth about events perhaps a millennium old, Homer's *Iliad* was nevertheless so immediate to the prince as to be a blueprint for his lifelong aspirations.

The epic poem covers a brief span toward the end of the ten-year-long war between Greece and Troy. (Other works, lost in antiquity, round out the story of the Trojan War, waged by the Greeks to retrieve Helen, an incomparable beauty married to King Menelaus of Sparta, who has been abducted by Paris, a Trojan prince.) The *Iliad*'s hero is brave and passionate Achilles, son of a Thessalian king and the sea goddess Thetis. Before he leaves for Troy, his mother warns him of two possible fates: He can go, win everlasting renown, and die young; or he can stay home and enjoy a long life. Without hesitation, he chooses glory over length of days.

Clad in golden armor forged by the god Hephaestus, Achilles soon proves himself the greatest of the Greek warriors. In battle, he is unbeatable. (As an infant, his mother had dipped him into the River Styx, whose waters rendered all parts they touched invulnerable—neglecting only the heel by which she held him.)

But as the *Iliad* opens, Achilles is retiring from the fray, angry because the Greek commander, Agamemnon, has claimed Achilles' war prize, a girl Achilles loves. As he sulks in his tent, the war turns in favor of the Trojans. Patroclus, Achilles' lover and dearest friend, begs to borrow his chariot and distinctive armor so that the Trojans, thinking him to be Achilles, might be driven back. Achilles agrees, and Patroclus leads a mighty charge before being killed by Prince Hector, foremost of the Trojan heroes.

Sick with grief and rage, Achilles returns to battle and seeks out Hector and kills him, even though he knows his fate is to die soon afterward. He then desecrates Hector's body, dragging it naked behind his chariot and refusing the sacred rite of burial. Eventually, grief-stricken Priam, the proud old king of Troy, dresses as a beggar and makes his way through the Greek lines to beg Achilles for his son's body. Achilles, remembering his own aged father and moved to tears, surrenders it, and the *Iliad* ends with Hector's funeral games.

Lost sources tell of Achilles' death. Shortly after Hector is killed, the cowardly Paris shoots a poisoned arrow from the walls of Troy, striking Achilles' unprotected heel and killing him.

To the Macedonians of Alexander's time, the Trojan War was not myth but history, its heroes real and their values still embraced. Achilles' passion and courage must have deeply stirred young Alexander's romantic nature, driving him to seek glory above all things and to accept as his own Achilles' credo: "Ever to strive to be the best." ▨

Above: Heroic Achilles is depicted in this detail from a fresco adorning a home in ancient Pompeii. A thirst for glory was not the only trait Alexander shared with his idol. Both were, at times, moody, sulky, and prone to deadly fits of rage.

Left: Grave dignity emanates from this marble bust of Homer, copied from an early third-century Greek original. Controversy has raged among academics for years over whether Homer actually wrote the *Iliad* and the other great epic attributed to him, the *Odyssey*.

Opposite: A painting by seventeenth-century Florentine artist Ciro Ferri shows the young Alexander poring over his *Iliad*. Among several anachronisms, the painting erroneously renders the prince's *Iliad* as a bound book, an invention that followed Alexander's time by about three centuries. His *Iliad* would have been in scroll form.

The romantic mysticism of Olympias was thus apparent in young Alexander, but so was the hardheaded pragmatism of Philip. Legend tells how the prince, only seven years old, capitalized with shrewd self-possession on a visit from Persian envoys. With the king absent, Alexander received the men politely and then began asking questions, not like a boy eager to hear of the magical wonders of the East, but like a general fishing for intelligence: How far was it to the Persian capital? How good were the roads that led there? And just how big was the Persian army? Years later, some of those present would have cause to remember the impressive boy when they faced the grown man in battle.

Alexander may have been a cherished prince, but he was by no means a pampered one. His raw intelligence and energy were in need of firm guidance, and his parents saw that he got it. His military training was early and ongoing, with the finest experts teaching him the use of sword, javelin, and bow. Nor were the gentler arts of music and poetry neglected; Alexander loved to read and proved to have a talent for the lyre. No doubt Philip was proud of his boy's proficiency with weapons, but he was less enthusiastic about the musical ability. Kings, he said, were lucky if they could find the time to listen to others play.

The remark may have stung, but it showed a confident superiority common to both father and son. As Alexander grew, he developed into such a swift runner that it was suggested that he compete in the Olympic Games (which by now accepted Macedonians). He would only be interested, he said, if there were other kings to compete against.

Below: Young Alexander tames the spirited Bucephalas in this bronze statuette from ancient Greece. The scale is probably fairly accurate, considering the small stature of the horses in the Greek world of Alexander's time.

Again like Philip, Alexander was from his earliest childhood a fine horseman, a fact that figures in the most famous childhood story of all: the taming of Bucephalas. The prince was perhaps eight or nine when a Thessalian horse-breeder offered to sell Philip a fine black stallion with a white blaze on his forehead. The horse, named Bucephalas for the ox-head brand he bore, was in his prime, a year or two younger than the boy. The asking price was also prime; thirteen talents was enough to keep a man in comfort for a lifetime. But the animal must have looked worth it, for Philip summoned his grooms to see how the stallion handled. Not well, it seemed: Bucephalas shied and reared and refused to be mounted, and the king ordered him taken away.

Alexander protested that an excellent horse was being lost because no one had the skill to master him. Amused, Philip asked his son if he thought he could do better. The prince replied that he could. And if he failed? Philip asked. Alexander answered that he would pay Bucephalas's price. The laughter was widespread, but the bet was made. The prince had noticed that the stallion had started at the sight of his own shadow, so the boy approached the horse, took his bridle, and turned his face toward the sun. For a time the two merely stood together, the boy stroking the horse, calming him. Then Alexander leaped on his back, and they galloped off across the plain. Thus began a deep and lasting attachment. Until his death at about thirty, Bucephalas would have no other rider, and he would always be Alexander's favorite mount.

When horse and rider returned to the king and his amazed retinue, Philip was nearly tearful with pride. "You'll have to find another kingdom," he said, kissing his son. "Macedon isn't going to be big enough for you."

There was love in the remark, to be sure, but perhaps something else as well. It must have occurred to Philip—and not for the last time—that this headstrong, fearless boy would be impatient for the throne himself, and sooner rather than later.

◆　◆　◆

Above: A student of the dance performs to the accompaniment of a flautist in this scene on a classical Attic red-figure vase.

Right: Reflecting the aesthetic values of his time, Renaissance artist Agostino Busti renders the famous horse-taming story in a more graceful, less muscular style. His marble relief was sculpted in the early sixteenth century.

Along with his general training, Alexander had in succession three tutors, and among them they disciplined his body, fed his fancies, and greatly expanded his mind. The first was Leonidas, an Epirot kinsman of Olympias. A tough old bird who brooked no nonsense, Leonidas helped assure the prince's Spartan austerity by rummaging through his clothes and bedding to make sure his mother had hidden no treats. Alexander would later say that the old man had his own ideas on how to feed a boy's appetite: a long night-march for breakfast and a light breakfast for supper. The discipline was not pleasant, but it was extremely effective. As a man, Alexander's physical endurance would border on the superhuman.

It is questionable whether he was grateful to Leonidas, but Alexander did not forget him. Once while sacrificing to the gods under his tutor's eye, the prince threw two handfuls of precious incense onto the altar fire. Leonidas was appalled. "When you've conquered the spice-bearing regions," he sneered, "you can throw away all the incense you like. Till then, don't waste it." Some fifteen years later, Alexander conquered Gaza, a major trading center for spice in the Middle East. Thereupon he sent more than fifteen tons of myrrh and frankincense—worth an unimaginable fortune—back to Macedon as a gift for Leonidas. With it came a terse admonition: Do not be stingy with the gods.

If the gift seemed to mark the giver as a man of splendid and selfless generosity, it also revealed something of his granite core. Alexander never forgot an insult, and if it took him years he would come up with the perfect, unassailable comeback. He may have been Greek on his mother's side, but in this respect he was wholly Macedonian.

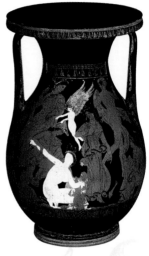

The second tutor was a sharp contrast to the first. Lysimachus of Acarnania was a toady and a flatterer, but he did encourage the young prince's grand dreams. He called the boy Achilles and himself Phoenix, the name of Achilles' aged mentor. Alexander must have enjoyed this fantasy, for he would one day take Lysimachus with him on his journey of conquest. He left Leonidas at home.

The prince, now into his teens, was growing into an accomplished and poised young man—and an extraordinarily handsome one. He was not very tall, but strongly built, graceful, and agile. His complexion was very fair, and his thick, tawny hair, often compared to a lion's mane, framed a face that (if later statues can be believed) was classically beautiful: The prominent brow was offset by large eyes, an aquiline nose, and a strong chin and jaw. The mouth was firm but sensuous, almost girlish. The youth, like the boy, was a masterpiece in the making. But he was still unfinished, and Philip felt it was time to hire another tutor to oversee his higher education.

There was no lack of aspirants for the post. Philip was by now a force in the Hellenic world, and he was known to be generous. But the king had his mind set on a boyhood friend whose father had been physician to his own father. As an adult, the young man had gone on to distinguish himself in Athens as Plato's star pupil. He was

Above: The sea nymph Thetis, mother of Achilles, tries to escape her mortal lover Peleus in this Athenian red-figure vase painting. Thetis was pursued by both Zeus and the sea god Poseidon before an oracle prophesied that she would bear a son greater than his father. To avoid this fate, the gods gave her to a mortal husband, King Peleus of Thessaly. She resisted wedding a mortal, and Peleus had to win her in a wrestling match in which she changed into fire, water, and a variety of animals in a futile effort to elude him. The prophecy, of course, came true.

Left: Some experts believe this bust of Alexander is the most true to life of all his portrait statuary. The bust is a Roman copy of a fourth-century BC carving.

not much to look at—thin, balding, and beady-eyed, deficiencies for which he overcompensated with foppish clothes and too many jewels. Nevertheless, his was the finest intellect of his time, perhaps of all time. His name was Aristotle.

He did not come cheap: Not only was his salary high and his perquisites lavish, but rumor had it that Philip lured him by agreeing to rebuild his hometown of Stageira, which the Macedonians had destroyed. If this were so, Alexander's education was likely the most expensive in history.

It is not known exactly what that education entailed, but the possibilities are nearly endless. Aristotle was a famous philosopher, of course, but he was also an authority on constitutional law, politics, poetry and rhetoric, astronomy and optics, metaphysics, medicine, zoology, and botany. These last two disciplines he pioneered, in fact; a tireless observer and experimenter, he was the father of the scientific method as it still exists today. He was also the father of logic and was thus as qualified to teach Alexander how to think as what to think.

It would seem that this collision of mature genius with emerging brilliance would have produced spectacular and enduring results, but there is only sketchy evidence that this was so. Aristotle may have been a reluctant teacher, since he considered the young to be mercurial and ruled by their emotions—unpromising clay to mold. "Their hopes fly as high as a drunkard's," he once wrote, "their memories are short. They are brave but conventional and therefore easily abashed. Unchastened by life, they prefer the noble to the useful: Their errors are on the grand scale, born of excess." Unlike the old, he added, "they think they know it all already." It may be telling that the words were written sometime after his stint as Alexander's tutor.

As for Alexander, there is little sign that Aristotelian philosophy ever informed his actions as an adult. Even so, the renowned tutor must at the very least have stimulated and brought to bloom the questing curiosity already present in the prince. Along with a keen appreciation of literature and the arts, Alexander would retain throughout his life an interest in the sciences, particularly in their practical application. On his Asian expedition he would take with him a subarmy of surveyors and collectors, people

who measured and mapped and explored, studied irrigation techniques and wasteland reclamation, who took samples of exotic plant and animal life and sent them back to Macedon for study.

• • •

Along with the best tutor, Philip supplied his son with the best setting and most congenial company. The king decided it would be good for the boy to get away from the distractions of the court—and perhaps from Olympias as well. Alexander's feelings for his father were a complicated blend of awe and envy, love and resentment. Philip was away from home more often than not, and when he was present, one can only imagine the mutual wariness, the flinty friction between two such extraordinary males at close quarters. But the ever-present Olympias was a different matter. Alexander loved his mother and trusted her, knowing that her fate was bound to his. And if her constant harping on his dynastic future might be tiresome at times, it also fed an appetite that was already ravenous.

In any case, the king sent the boy and his teacher off to one of the loveliest spots in Macedon, the Precinct of the Nymphs at Mieza, part of the fabled Gardens of Midas. Located in the foothills of the Bermius Mountains, the valley offered lush orchards and vineyards, shady promenades and waterfalls—the perfect spot for study and contemplation. For company, Philip sent along several other young men, sons of the Macedonian elite, to study under Aristotle. All friends of the prince, they were an exceptional assemblage. There were other future kings among them, and almost all the youths would become part of Alexander's inner circle in years to come. Also among them was the young man who was, and would always be, the most important person in Alexander's life.

Hephaestion was his name, and he and the prince had known each other since childhood. They were lovers, but the sexual aspect of their bond was almost incidental to the profound emotional tie that for both was lifelong. Hephaestion was Patroclus to Alexander's Achilles: his closest companion, advisor, and confidant, the one person he relied on to love him unselfishly, for himself alone.

The fact that their relationship was homosexual would not have occasioned any opprobrium in their culture. Macedonians and Greeks regarded same-sex attachments as a normal phase for young men, and for older ones a natural enough adjunct to sex with women. Like Philip, Alexander would be bisexual, though the son would skew more toward the homosexual end of the scale, to the extent that he was sexual at all. Alexander would always be extremely fastidious about physical intimacy, perhaps in reaction to Philip's goatish indulgence, or perhaps because it was just his nature. His interest in women was late blooming and

Above: No portrait of Hephaestion has been identified with certainty, but this large, bronze head attributed to the sculptor Polycleitus is believed to depict Alexander's handsome, lifelong companion.

Opposite: A bit overgrown but still inviting, the Mieza landscape where Alexander and his companions walked with Aristotle is known today as the Gardens of the Muses.

tepid at best, and it took an extraordinary person of either sex to rouse his passions. Noting his indifference to women, Philip and Olympias once hired a beautiful Thessalian courtesan to initiate him. She failed. "Sex and sleep alone make me conscious that I am mortal," Alexander once remarked. He did not much care for such reminders.

Whatever his sexual appetites (or lack thereof), there was nothing effeminate about the prince. He was a warrior born and bred, and had a passion for glory on a Homeric scale that was the ruling star of his life. Glory meant battle and conquest, and the time had come for Alexander to start down that road.

◆　◆　◆

During the three years the prince spent with Aristotle, Philip's fortunes in Greece were on the decline. Athens, believing rightly that the king was maneuvering for control of her vital grain route from the Black Sea through the Hellespont, was rallying support from other city-states to oppose him. In addition, the Athenians had convinced the Great King of Persia—Artaxerxes Ochus, at the time—to help finance a war against Macedon. Philip decided to lead an expedition to choke off two important ports leading to the Black Sea. Before leaving, he called Alexander home from Mieza and made him regent. The prince was then sixteen years old.

Almost at once, Alexander proved that youth was no barrier to his leading men into combat. He organized a lightning assault against a bellicose tribe on the border of Thrace, a neighboring kingdom under Macedonian control. The raid was a complete success, and the prince captured the tribe's chief settlement and boldly exercised the kingly perquisite of renaming it after himself: Alexandropolis. Of far greater importance was the fact that Alexander had shown for the first time—as he would time and again—that he could command unquestioning allegiance from men much older and more experienced than he. It was more than a matter of rank or even ability; there was something in his very presence and bearing that marked him as a leader.

Unfortunately, Philip's campaign in the north was faring less well, and he returned to Macedon prepared to stake everything on one monumental throw of the dice: force a decisive land battle against Athens and her allies. To that end he began leading his army down through central Greece. Athens, still a great sea power, unwisely chose to try

Above: Darius's predecessor, the Great King Artaxerxes Ochus II, is depicted in this etching. Artaxerxes was killed by his own grand vizier, who then installed Darius on the Persian throne. Apparently more wary than grateful at such treachery, Darius had the murderer killed.

Left: The Lion of Chaeronea still watches over the ancient battlefield where Philip defeated the Athenians and Thebans. The marble monument marks the mass grave of the Theban Band, famed in antiquity for valor. The Band was made up of 150 pairs of lovers sworn to protect one another unto death. Most died fighting at Chaeronea. Capering across the field after the battle, Philip stopped short when he came to their corpses and began to weep.

to stop him on land, thus playing directly into his hands. In the late summer of 338 BC, allied Greek forces led by Athens and Thebes faced off against the Macedonians near the sleepy little town of Chaeronea in central Greece.

The tactics were classically Philip's. He commanded on the right at the head of his elite Shield Bearers brigade. His center, the indomitable Macedonian phalanx, was angled back from the opposing Greek line. To the far left was the Macedonian cavalry, led by the crown prince, who at eighteen was entrusted with the pivotal element of his father's battle plan. Philip and his men engaged the enemy first and soon feigned retreat, backing up slowly and methodically, still facing front. The Athenian troops of the center took the bait, drifting more and more to their left to be in on the kill. Finally, fatally, a gap opened between the Athenians and their most formidable allies, the fabled Theban Sacred Band, which stood its ground.

Into this opening rushed the wedge of Macedonian cavalry, with Alexander galloping in the lead. Soldiers of the phalanx poured in behind the cavalry, and the battle turned into a rout. Thousands of Greeks were killed, thousands more captured.

In victory Philip was magnanimous, and as always, practical. He astonished the Athenians with his leniency (why risk rousing that troublesome navy?), returning the ashes of their dead for burial, releasing the captives without ransom, and promising not to invade Athens. He was much harsher with Thebes, garrisoning the city, breaking up her holdings in Boeotia, and demanding ransom for the Theban prisoners. The difference in Philip's mind was clear: Thebes had been his ally before aligning with Athens, his declared enemy.

THE MACEDONIAN ARMY

However gifted, Alexander would never have become "the Great" without the army that his father created, the finest the world had known to that time. Its basic units—cavalry and infantry—were staples, but the way they were disciplined, equipped, and combined under Philip made them unique.

As usual in antiquity, the cavalry was made up of landed gentry with the wherewithal to outfit themselves with horses and equipment. In Macedon, these nobles were often on familiar terms with the king, bound by kinship or friendship, and were known as the Companions. They numbered around six hundred when Philip became king, but as his expansionism brought more territory and thus more landowners and more horsemen, the Companion Cavalry broadened into thousands. All were excellent riders—necessarily so, since saddles and stirrups were unknown to them. They essentially rode bareback, with only a blanket separating them from the small, stocky mounts that they guided with only their knees and a bridle. The cavalrymen wore metal helmets and breastplates of either metal or leather, and their weapon of choice was a long thrusting spear.

Above: Although small, the domed Macedonian shield served to protect the heart while allowing an infantryman maximum mobility.

Right: Equipment from the tomb of a fourth-century BC Greek warrior includes a heavy bronze breastplate, a belt, and other items.

Yet it was not the cavalry but the infantry that was Philip's landmark contribution. In his day, Greek hoplites (infantrymen) were usually citizen soldiers. They underwent some military training as an obligation of citizenship, and they had often acquitted themselves well in the past, fighting in densely packed phalanxes (the Greek word for "fingers") with spears and short swords. But the hoplite phalanx had drawbacks: The men were weighed down by heavy armor and enormous shields, and they were not always available for ongoing duty. Many were shepherds or farmers; tied to the land, they had to leave the fighting to plant or harvest, thus rendering war a seasonal pursuit. Among the Greeks, only Sparta, with a huge slave-labor force, had the means to maintain a standing army.

But Philip—using mineral wealth, plunder, and tribute—created a professional infantry of his own, one far superior to Sparta's. His chief innovations were to lighten the infantry's defensive armor, making it much more maneuverable, and to equip it with a superior offensive weapon.

The Macedonian shield was round and small, only some eighteen inches across and strapped to the left shoulder, and the infantry body armor was either pared down or eliminated. The distinctive new weapon for offense was the fearsome *sarissa*. This was a pike, as long as eighteen feet, made of two lengths of tough cornel wood joined by a bronze band. Broad at the base and tipped with a foot-long blade, the sarissa was twice as long as the standard Greek sword and could thus skewer

an enemy before he could get within stabbing range. The sarissa made the phalanx a bristling hedgehog on defense, and on offense an unstoppable juggernaut.

Philip renamed his infantry the "Macedonian Foot Companions," an enhanced status. The Companions were full-time soldiers who were disciplined to a fine edge, drilled constantly, and trained to march thirty miles at a stretch over any terrain, in any weather, and to live off the land. Distance and season were no barriers. Before Philip, the infantry had fought in files of ten; he changed their formation to multiples of eight. They could accommodate terrain by marching in columns, squares, or wedges, widening their front by thinning to eight-man depth, or narrowing it by increasing the depth to sixteen, thirty-two, or more.

To the Companions and phalanx—and to the archers and slingers who provided what there was of artillery in ancient times—Philip introduced an important extra element, the Royal Shield Bearers. Some three thousand strong, these special infantrymen were more heavily armed in pitched battle and were used to protect the undefended right side of the phalanx and to link the phalanx with the cavalry. Shedding their heavy gear, they could also serve as raiders, commandos, and shock troops, and they were among the king's most versatile and reliable men.

For all the talent and labor it took to create the elements of his army, Philip's genius shone brightest in the way he combined them, uniting them tactically in a way that was almost balletic. Traditionally, Hellenic generals had aligned their strongest troops against the opponent's weaker side. But Philip was among the earliest leaders to understand the principle of economy of force: The most efficient way to win a battle is to first dispense with the enemy's strength. He would begin a battle with his line of infantry angled back, the cavalry held in reserve on the right side, under the king's direct command. As the front of the phalanx engaged the enemy infantry, the opposing line inevitably drifted to concentrate its strength at the point of contact. Sooner or later the drift would open a gap in the enemy line, and into this fatal opening would gallop the Companion Cavalry in wedge formation, apex first, scattering the leading ranks of defenders and then wheeling around to harry opponents in the rear as the rest of the phalanx pressed forward in the horsemen's wake.

It was a tactic that served Philip well, and one that Alexander would tune to perfect pitch, especially in the timing and effectiveness of the cavalry charge. This crucial maneuver relied heavily on the leader's dash and flair, and in that department Alexander was unrivaled. The fact that the father created the tool that the son would use with such success in no way diminishes Alexander's status as history's greatest warrior. Still, he owed Philip much, as he himself was always uncomfortably aware. ▨

One could be gracious to a defeated foe, but traitors deserved the worst. It was an example Alexander would often follow. A momentarily grateful Athens made Philip and Alexander honorary citizens and commissioned statues of them. Philip sent envoys to escort home the ashes of the dead. Alexander was among them; it was his only visit to the once-great cradle of Greek culture.

With Athens submissive and Thebes neutralized, almost all of Greece fell in behind Philip. He made separate treaties with the various city-states, then called a general peace conference at Corinth. Sparta was the only absentee. The conclave would continue for some time, but behind polite language and meaningless concessions, its outcome was inevitable. Philip was the leader of Greece, and his new allies were to help him in the upcoming venture toward which his entire career had pointed: the invasion of Asia. The Greeks were not happy with the arrangement. Beneath the public kowtowing they hated Philip, and they would hate Alexander after him. For the moment, however, there was no choice but to dance to Macedon's tune.

Understandably, Philip was euphoric in the wake of Chaeronea. About a month after the battle, he commissioned at Olympia a building called the Philippeum, a circular structure housing statues of himself, his parents, and Olympias and Alexander. Within a stone's throw of the great Olympic temples of Zeus and Hera, this shrine seemed to proclaim semidivine

Above: The foundation of the Philippeum, Philip's temple to himself and his family, still stands at Olympia, home of the ancient Olympic Games. The Philippeum was commissioned by Philip in 338 BC and completed during Alexander's reign. Within the circle of stones are pedestals that once held statues of the royal family.

Opposite: Little more than columns remain of what was once the temple of the goddess Hera at Olympia. A larger temple, sacred to her husband, Zeus, once stood near it.

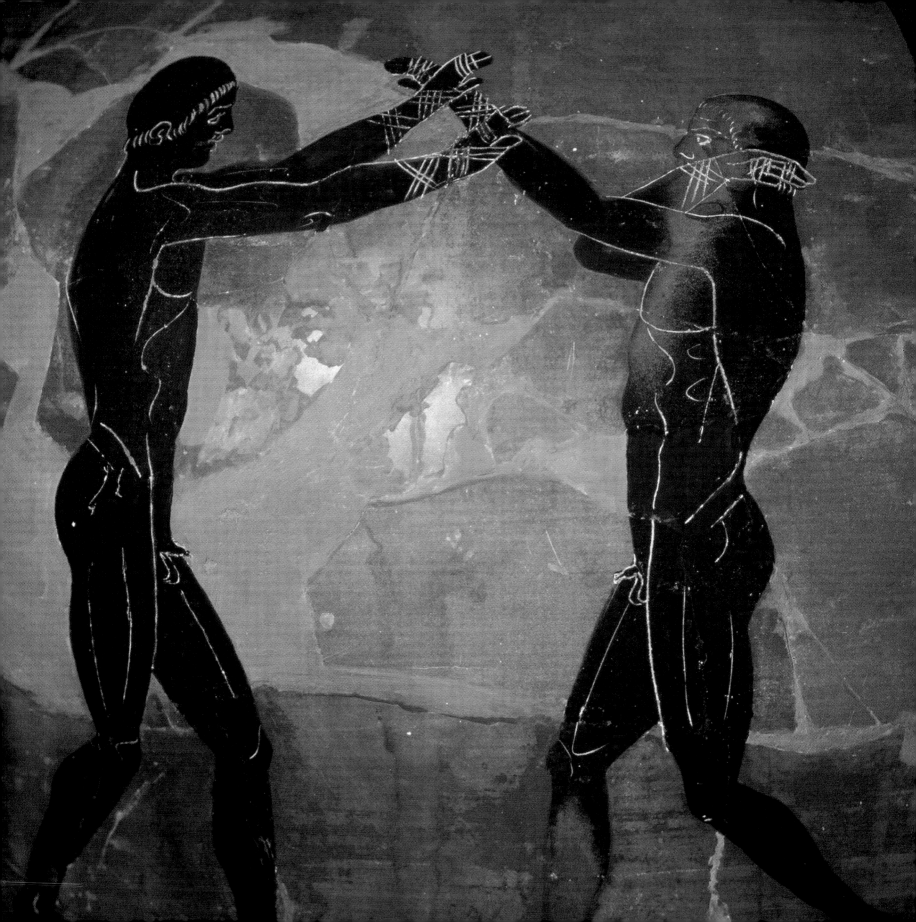

status for the king and his family. It was an odd gesture for a realist like Philip. Perhaps he thought his own quasi-religious cult would be politically useful; perhaps he really believed he had earned it. He had reached a pinnacle, and he stood atop it mighty and godlike. On such a peak it must have been easy to forget that linchpin of Greek tragedy, hubris: Pride that dares the gods invites their wrath.

◆ ◆ ◆

Back in Macedon, Philip decided to marry again. There had already been one wife after Olympias—a Thracian princess—and that marriage had apparently occasioned no objection from either Olympias or Alexander. This time, however, the king's intended was a Macedonian girl, an aristocrat of impeccable lineage named Cleopatra. It was said to be a love match; Philip, now in his forties, was smitten with a girl less than half his age. He probably was, but that was no reason for marriage had her connections not been as attractive as her person.

Cleopatra was the niece of Attalus, a proven and popular general who figured prominently in Philip's invasion plans. What mattered to Alexander about the union was that any son it produced would be pure Macedonian, not half Greek as he was. This, he seemed to feel, might bode ill for his succession—and though probably proud of his Greek heritage, Alexander might have worried that his countrymen preferred one of their own. Nevertheless, the cause for his anxiety is hard to understand (though one suspects Olympias's fine hand). Philip had carefully groomed him for nearly twenty years to inherit the crown. But Alexander would almost surely be going to Asia with his father, and in war anything could happen. It was only prudent for Philip to produce more Argeads, if possible, before setting out. Even so, tensions were running unusually high in the palace at Pella as the wedding approached.

They came to a head at the wedding feast. As customary on such occasions, the celebrants grew drunker and drunker as the evening wore on. They were very drunk by the time Attalus staggered to his feet and proposed a toast: Macedonians should pray to the gods that this marriage might produce a legitimate successor to the kingdom.

Outraged at this crude and unmistakable insult, Alexander leaped to his feet.

"Are you calling me a bastard?" he screamed, hurling his goblet at Attalus.

Attalus threw his own cup at the prince. Then Philip lurched forward, drawing his sword. He tottered a few drunken steps on his lame leg, then fell. Alexander looked down with utter contempt at his father, sprawled on the floor.

"That, gentlemen, is the man who has been preparing to cross from Europe into Asia," the prince sneered, "and he cannot even make it from one couch to the next!" With that, he

Above: Crowned with laurel, the god Apollo appears in relief on this gold coin minted during Philip's reign.

Opposite: A detail from an amphora dating to the Greek archaic period shows combat between a pair of boxers.

Previous spread: Rocky outcroppings rise behind the ruins of the temple of Apollo at Corinth. The temple was built during the sixth century BC.

stormed out into the night, collected his mother, and left the kingdom. He took Olympias to her kin in Epirus, then continued north to spend several months of sullen exile with the Illyrians.

Back in Pella, Philip continued planning for his Asian expedition and awaiting the birth of his first child by Cleopatra. It was born in the summer of 337 BC: a girl. The king could no longer wait to see if his wife might yet produce an alternate heir. It would be pure folly, Philip well knew, to set out for Asia leaving behind a man as discontented and dangerous as Alexander to threaten his base in Macedon. He summoned his son home, presumably with reassurances that Alexander was still his chosen heir. Ostensibly the rift was healed, but mistrust and resentment still simmered.

Above: Priests relay a petitioner's question to the Pythia at Delphi.

They soon erupted again. Philip assented to a marriage between his son Arrhidaeus to the daughter of a Carian prince named Pixodarus. Caria was a Persian satrapy in Asia Minor, potentially a useful ally in the coming invasion. Arrhidaeus was not much of a chip to play politically, so the arrangement was an obvious bargain. (Philip would never have wasted the crown prince on a fairly minor alliance.) Nevertheless, Alexander, illogically, construed the deal as a threat and sent an envoy to Caria to offer himself in Arrhidaeus's stead. When Philip learned of this he was furious. There would be no such marriage, of course; his alliance was ruined, and for nothing. He let Alexander off with a tongue-lashing but sent several of his friends who had known about the Carian offer into exile.

◆　◆　◆

Bad blood still quietly flowed as Philip arranged yet another marriage, an important one. Some time before, Philip had helped depose the old king of Epirus and enthrone in his stead Olympias's younger brother, also named Alexander. Philip now proposed to marry this Alexander to his daughter Cleopatra. That the groom and bride were uncle and niece was evidently not considered a barrier.

By now Philip had dispatched an advance force of ten thousand men across the Hellespont, and he planned to follow soon with the main army. All was in readiness: He had sent an envoy to the Delphic Oracle to be sure the gods favored his venture and had received auspicious tidings—or so it seemed to him. The bull is garlanded, the Pythia had said. The sacrifice is at hand. Surely this meant that Persia's Great King would be the sacrificial bull, and Philip himself the sacrificer. So the wedding would be his swan song before leaving, and he meant to make it spectacular. Friends and dignitaries from all over Greece were invited for days of lavish feasting and ceremony at the ancient capital of Aegae.

It was arranged that the crown prince would be conspicuously present at the festival, for once again he seemed unassailably the heir apparent, since Philip's most recent child

was a girl. For the second day of the wedding festivities, Philip had engineered a particularly impressive event, a procession in which he would march with the two Alexanders, the crown prince and his new son-in-law. They would be proceeded by a ceremonial parade of thirteen magnificent effigies representing the twelve Olympian gods and, in that most august company, Philip himself. It was another hint at his assumption of divine status.

The great day came, and Philip, clad all in ceremonial white, began marching forward with his son and son-in-law. The king's bodyguards had been instructed to stay out of sight: Philip did not want to appear before all of Greece as a tyrant in need of protection. But one of them lingered nearby. The young man's name was Pausanias, and he had once been Philip's lover. After being discarded for a new favorite, also named Pausanias, he had angrily denounced his successor as, among other things, a paid tart. Stung, the new favorite behaved rashly in battle to prove his manhood and managed to get himself killed. Thus began a blood feud, among the most time-honored of Macedonian traditions. As fate would have it, the dead Pausanias was a kinsman of Attalus, Philip's general and new father-in-law. Attalus took fierce vengeance at this affront to his kin. He invited the offending Pausanias to a dinner party, got him drunk, had him raped by all present, then turned him over to servants to repeat the outrage. Pausanias went to Philip for justice. The king was sympathetic but did nothing; his interests lay with his general.

Now, watching as his betrayer marched in glorious celebration, Pausanias drew out his dagger. Before the horrified eyes of hundreds of onlookers, he rushed forward and plunged it into Philip's chest, then fled toward waiting horses.

As the king lay on the ground, his life's blood seeping away, there was an instant of shocked silence. Then the tumult began. People shouted and surged to and fro while above them all the twelve great Olympians gazed with bland, indifferent eyes at the one who had aspired to join their number, the matter of his own immortality now, it seemed, decided. The Pythia had spoken truly: The sacrifice had indeed been at hand. The king had merely fatally misconstrued who was the sacrifice, and who the sacrificer.

The great Philip was dead. His son was now Alexander III, king of Macedon. ◉

THE DEATH OF PHILIP

Was it conspiracy or a lone assassin?

Above: This gold ossuary was found in the ruins of the royal Macedonian tombs at Vergina. It once held the remains of a male of the Argead line, possibly Philip's elder son, Arrhidaeus, half brother of Alexander.

Right: A detail from a silver jar also found at Vergina shows a young Macedonian royal wearing a lion-skin headdress, symbolic of the Argead dynasty. The face may represent Alexander himself.

In ancient times, as now, the assassination of a great man was apt to spawn a host of conspiracy theories, and so it was with the death of Philip. A spur to speculation was the report that the assassin Pausanias fled toward waiting "horses"—plural. Who provided them, and who besides Pausanias was supposed to ride them? Did the killing involve the connivance of the Persians or the Athenians (both notions plausible enough) or some other enemy, foreign or domestic? Most intriguing—then and now—was the theory that the masterminds behind the regicide were Philip's wife, or son, or both.

Suspicion fell immediately on Olympias, and she did not discourage it. It was said that while Pausanias's body still hung in disgrace on a public gibbet, she placed a golden crown on its head and shortly thereafter burned the body atop her husband's remains. Supposedly, she even dedicated the killer's fatal dagger to the god Apollo. These public, flagrant acts suggest that she, playing on Pausanias's anger, had incited him to kill Philip, motivated by her own lust for vengeance.

According to this theory, Philip had repudiated Olympias, perhaps suspecting that she—and possibly Alexander as well—was plotting against him. Having recently married young Cleopatra, the king may have gambled that his new wife would produce an heir, rendering Olympias and Alexander superfluous. Outraged at the insult and the threat to her son's succession, Olympias would have arranged Philip's murder and then gloried in the deed, knowing that with Alexander on the throne, no one could touch her. But her own actions comprise the only evidence against her and, since Philip's death did assure Alexander's kingship, she could have celebrated the murder without having caused it. The matter remains one of history's imponderables.

Against Alexander there is no evidence at all, except for the tantalizing truth that he had the most to gain from Philip's death. The crown itself must have been enticing, for Alexander was not a man to long endure subservience to anyone. Besides, Philip's demise would have ended at last the constant friction between father and son, exacerbated by Alexander's nagging doubts about his succession.

More significant by far, however, is the fact that Philip was poised to thwart the thirst for glory that was his son's guiding star. The impending Asian crusade promised to be a crucible of legends, a once-in-a-lifetime setting for heroic deeds. Alexander had long complained to his friends that Philip, with all his accomplishments, was leaving him no brilliant feats of his own to display. When they replied that Philip was acquiring everything for him, he retorted, "What use are possessions to me if I achieve nothing?" What if Alexander went to Asia only as the inglorious second-in-command? Worse, what if Philip left him behind in Macedon as regent? The prospect must have seemed intolerable. With Philip out of the way, nothing would stand between Alexander and his chance for greatness.

On the other hand, the Hellenic world regarded parricide as among the most terrible and unnatural of crimes—hardly a promising platform for launching a glorious career. Moreover, whatever their conflicts and jealousies, there was a bond between Philip and Alexander, of blood and of the comradeship of warriors. By some accounts, Alexander had saved Philip's life at Chaeronea. On balance, it strains credulity to posit that the son then became the father's murderer.

In any event, soon after Philip's death, Alexander had two young highland nobles executed for complicity in the murder. The reasoning went that Philip's marriage to a well-connected lowlander and his repudiation of Olympias (whose homeland of Epirus had close ties to the Macedonian highlands) left the highlanders fearful of diminished influence at court, and for this they killed the king. Later, Alexander would accuse Darius and the Persians of instigating the assassination, though it is doubtful that he truly believed this.

In the tangle of passion and politics surrounding Philip and Alexander, the whole truth about the king's assassination may be lost forever. Still, history must favor the verdict of Pausanias as the lone assassin, for this is the version supplied by the only contemporary of the crime who wrote a reliable account of it. In a general discussion of regicide in his work *Politics*, Aristotle ascribes the crime to one abused and disaffected young man. The great philosopher was, of course, intimately familiar with Macedonian politics and court life, and he knew all the principal players in the dynastic drama. Writing after the death of both Philip and Alexander, he had no particular ax to grind, and there is no reason to doubt his conclusions, however fascinating and sensational the theories to the contrary. ▩

Above: Some of the artifacts excavated at Vergina were fairly plain, such as this simple bronze lantern, while others were remarkably ornate.

Left: This elaborate *gorytos*, or case for carrying a bow and quiver, was made of gilded silver. It features an intricate repoussé depiction of the capture of a city. Both the gorytos and the lantern above date from the late fourth century BC.

CHAPTER TWO

[AGE 20–22   YEAR 335–333 BC]

THE KING

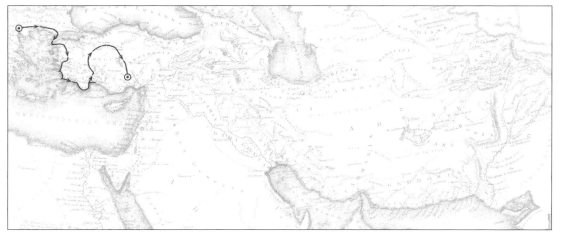

Above: A third-century BC bust of Alexander in the style of the sculptor Leochares shows the king in a pose popular in his portrait statues: head tilted slightly upward and to the left. Whether this attitude was aesthetically satisfying to artists or resulted from some actual physical quirk of Alexander's is unknown. Whatever the case, the pose set a long-lasting style for sculptural subjects.

Above: A relief of Alexander's classic profile adorns a medallion by Ohnmacht von Landolin.

Opposite: In the guise of a Christian prince, Alexander rides astride a leopard on this thirteenth-century stained glass window in a Cistercian church in Heiligenkreuz, Austria. Medieval romances transformed the king into a model of chivalrous knighthood.

WHATEVER ALEXANDER FELT on witnessing Philip's murder, he lost no time mourning. The dead king's corpse was not even cold before his son picked up the reins of monarchy and took them firmly in hand. If there was grief, doubtless it was swept aside in the flood of joy Alexander must have felt at being at last his own man, poised on the threshold of the glorious destiny he had long envisioned.

Besides, there was no time to be lost. The death of an extraordinary leader like Philip was bound to leave chaos in its wake—rebellions in Greece, certainly, and to the north, the resumption of the age-old predations of the border tribes. At twenty, Alexander faced challenges similar to those confronting his father more than two decades before: He must crush sedition at home, secure his borders, and quell

Opposite: This map shows the early stages of Alexander's Asian campaign. He traveled eastward from his homeland, crossing the Hellespont (now the Dardenelles) to begin a long, looping journey through Asia Minor (modern Turkey).

Below: Head of Alexander, first century BC

dissent in Greece. Only then could he look beyond to Asia and the dream of conquest that had been Philip's and was now his own.

His first task entailed securing support from the Macedonian army and feudal barons, and he took a major stride in that direction at once. As soon as Philip's body was removed from the theater at Aegae, Alexander was presented to the army as the new king by one of the most influential men in Macedon, Antipater. A general and one of Philip's mainstays for many years, Antipater had been Alexander's advisor during the prince's regency.

After the ceremony, Alexander addressed such Macedonian common folk as could be assembled. He promised that his father's policies would continue, and—to predictable applause—he vowed to exempt the general populace from taxation. He spent the rest of the day receiving foreign delegates, exacting assurances that the leadership of Greece would devolve upon him. He also recalled his close friends from exile to help form the nucleus of his new administration.

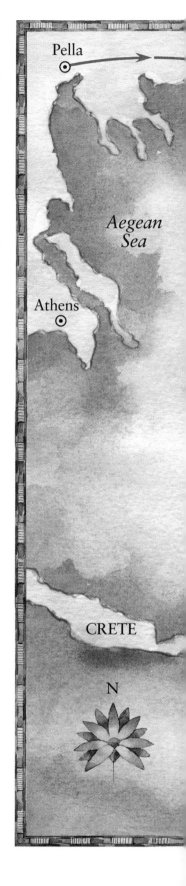

It seemed a good beginning, but Alexander must have been acutely aware of danger on all sides, beginning close to home. There were, after all, two other Argead males who might conceivably contest his right to the throne. Arrhidaeus was not much of a threat, but there remained Amyntas, Alexander's cousin, the son of Philip's slain elder brother, King Perdiccas II. Some five years older than Alexander, Amyntas had lived peaceably enough at court over the years, never asserting a claim to the crown. Even so, he was an obvious rallying point for dissenters, foreign and domestic, bent on throttling Philip's cub before he could begin to roar. Amyntas would need watching. For the moment, though, Alexander left him unmolested. The new king was mindful of his public image, and the spectacle of another Macedonian dynastic bloodletting would not play well in Greece. Besides, he had more pressing concerns.

Among these were two men who, though away with Philip's advance force in Asia Minor, might still cloud his horizon. One was a wily old survivor named Parmenio, commander of the advance expeditionary force, once described by Philip as the only general he had ever needed. Now in his mid-sixties, Parmenio was a legend to his troops and a power among the lowland barons, and to Alexander his support was pivotal.

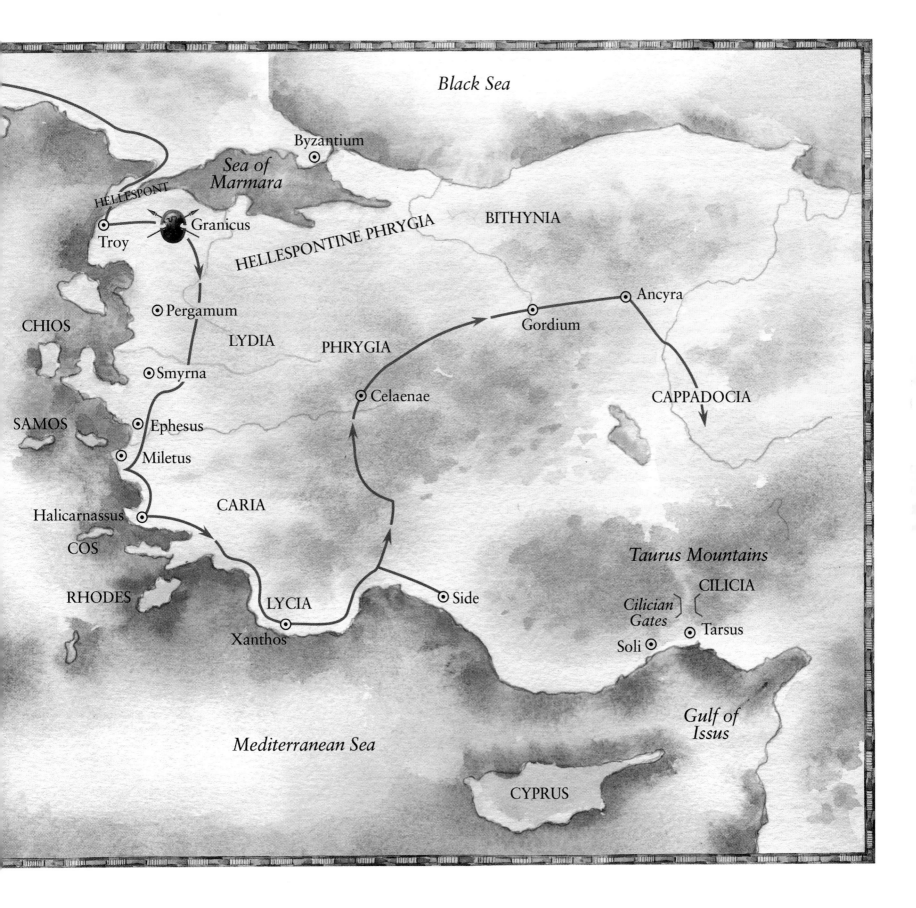

Black Sea

Byzantium

Sea of Marmara

HELLESPONT

Troy

Granicus

HELLESPONTINE PHRYGIA

BITHYNIA

Ancyra

Pergamum

Gordium

CHIOS

LYDIA

PHRYGIA

CAPPADOCIA

Smyrna

Celaenae

SAMOS

Ephesus

Miletus

CARIA

Taurus Mountains

Halicarnassus

CILICIA

COS

Cilician Gates

RHODES

LYCIA

Side

Tarsus

Soli

Xanthos

Gulf of Issus

Mediterranean Sea

CYPRUS

THE ATHENIAN PROBLEM

Right: King Oedipus of Thebes embraces his daughter Antigone in a sculpture by nineteenth-century French artist Jean-Baptiste Hugues. The doomed pair are central characters in the Oedipus Cycle, a trilogy by the great Athenian playwright Sophocles. Athenians loved the theater and held annual contests for playwrights. Those competing during the city's fifth-century BC heyday included some of the greatest in history.

During the reigns of both Philip and Alexander, no Greek adversary was a more troublesome thorn in Macedon's side than Athens. The two foes resorted to arms only once, at Chaeronea. But even afterward, thoroughly thrashed in battle and forced into fawning alliance, Athens bubbled with venom toward the Macedonians, and rebellion was never far from the surface.

A prime reason for the ongoing ill will was Demosthenes, Athens' most legendary orator. Born into rather modest circumstances and cursed with a speech defect, Demosthenes nevertheless aspired to be a great and influential speaker, and he drove himself toward that end with admirable tenacity. The famous story of his practicing oratory on the sea-shore with pebbles in his mouth is probably apocryphal, but he must have endured some equally stringent discipline, for in time he became an extremely effective molder and swayer of opinion. He required only a volatile political issue on which to peg his hard-won talent, and for this the Macedonians were tailor-made.

Behind the scenes Demosthenes sabotaged Philip's diplomatic overtures and saw to it that any offer of friendship was rebuffed, and in the Athenian assembly he railed against the Macedonian king relentlessly and well enough to give posterity a new word: "philippic," meaning a passionate speech of denunciation. He decried Philip's autocratic and expansionist public life and his untidy and licentious private one. There was a pro-Macedonian faction in Athens (its numbers included the aged Isocrates, who saw greatness in Philip and urged him to lead Greece in a war of vengeance against the Persians), but Demosthenes usually managed to override it. After Philip's death, he scarcely missed a beat before turning his vitriol on Alexander. He characterized the new king as an omen-ridden young buffoon and—in a barb that must have hit home Demosthenes called him "Margites," the protagonist of a mock-Homeric work that caricatured Achilles. The

Given this noisy nuisance, and Athens' persistent intransigence, it seems remarkable that Macedon refrained from dealing the city the same fate that Alexander would inflict on Thebes. There were practical reasons for the restraint, however, not least among them the still-formidable Athenian navy. Athens had built her empire with her ships and their well-trained crews, and those ships remained potentially dangerous or useful, depending on who could command them.

But there were psychological reasons as well. Athens may have been a century past her golden apogee, but in her prime she had been the city that turned back the Persians at Marathon and Salamis; she had been, too, the city of Socrates, of the great statesman Pericles, and of matchless art and sublime literature, including the immortal plays of Aeschylus, Sophocles, Euripides, and Aristophanes. As surely as Macedon was the Hellenic world's Balkan backwater, Athens remained its cultured and cosmopolitan heart. Philip was all too aware of this, and though he regarded Athenian democracy as absurdly cumbersome and most of its practitioners as venal and silly, he could not help regarding the city itself with reluctant awe.

Alexander, of course, was a much harder man to awe. Even so, he shared a modicum of his father's reverence for the city's history and achievements and so stayed his lethal hand. Like forlorn suitors, both kings seemed to hope that Athens would someday come around. But Philip died before he could win her; and Alexander, leaving her far behind, would eventually cease to care. ▨

implication, of course, was that Alexander was laughable in his well-known pretensions to rival the greatest of Greek heroes.

Demosthenes was badly flawed. He was a physical coward and greedy to boot, and the disclosure that he was taking bribes from the Persians landed him in a public scandal. But he had an uncanny gift for surviving setbacks and regaining lost ground, and it seemed that nothing would permanently shut him up.

Serving under Parmenio was Attalus, the powerful and ambitious general who had publicly called Alexander a bastard and who could expect little favor from him now. Attalus was Parmenio's son-in-law. If the two united to oppose the new king, they could cause serious trouble. Athens, smelling blood, set about trying to make sure they would.

The Athenians, so lately Philip's sycophantic allies, had greeted the news of his death with a day of public thanksgiving. Soon after, Demosthenes wrote to Parmenio and Attalus, promising Athens' support if the two made war on Alexander. (Attalus jumped at the chance; Parmenio bided his time.) Alexander was probably unaware of the plot in its early stages, but he certainly knew that insurrection seethed in Athens and was threatening to become general throughout Greece. Thebes, Sparta, Argos, Arcadia, and several other areas were already in active revolt.

With so many threats unresolved, Alexander's Macedonian advisors counseled him to keep a low profile for a while and leave the Greeks alone. The advice fell on deaf ears. Reasoning rightly that an early sign of weakness would guarantee his downfall, he declared he would confront the situation with "courage and audacity" and soon set out at the head of an elite corps, riding south into the heart of Greece.

The speed and daring of this ploy were enough in themselves to make it a success. Not a battle was fought; the mere threat of one was enough. Envoys from the various states arrived along Alexander's line of march, promising loyalty. Even the Thebans, who had expelled Philip's garrison as soon as they heard of his death, looked down at the battle-hardened troops beneath the city walls and promptly capitulated. Forty miles to the southeast, a panicky Athens followed suit. Demosthenes, who had recently assured his citizens that Alexander was a foolish young twit who could be safely ignored, was included in the delegation sent to placate him. (The great orator traveled only a few miles before prudently deciding to return home.)

These developments were closely watched by the Macedonian high command across the Hellespont. Noting Athens' submission, an unnerved Attalus had Demosthenes' letters delivered to Alexander, along with an earnest declaration of support. Alexander had Attalus killed. Parmenio, who knew a winner when he saw one, raised no objection to his son-in-law's execution. He cast his lot with Alexander, though not without a price: For years to come, the army's highest echelon would be liberally sprinkled with his kin.

Alexander had cause for satisfaction. King for only two months, he had swiftly shown himself a force to be reckoned with, both to the Greeks and to any possible Macedonian dissenters. Now, like his father before him, he summoned delegates from the city-states to

Above: Alexander's archenemy Attalus is depicted in this second-century BC sculpture. Through his connections to the army and to his niece, Philip's widow, Attalus may have hoped to control the throne if he could have Alexander deposed or killed.

Opposite: Like the rest of the building, the west face of the Parthenon shows centuries of damage, but the edifice remains structurally intact. The scaffolding behind the columns is part of a repair effort that has been ongoing for centuries. The Doric masterpiece was built during the fifth century BC at the height of Athenian prestige and power.

THE DELPHIC ORACLE

What really happened at Delphi?

The shrine of Apollo at Delphi was home to the most renowned soothsayers of antiquity, a succession of women each known as the Delphic Oracle or the Pythia. Though the priestess's pronouncements were famously enigmatic, she was believed to utter only divine truth. Philip had been her generous patron, and Alexander, on becoming king, was eager to seek her out.

Thus, on returning to Macedon from the meeting of the Hellenic League at Corinth, he stopped off at Delphi, probably hoping for auguries regarding the future of the Asian campaign. But it was late November, and as a matter of religious custom the Oracle did not prophesy from mid-November through mid-February. She refused to make an exception, even for Alexander.

Undaunted, the young king entered her dwelling, grabbed her, and began unceremoniously dragging her into the shrine. "Young man, you are invincible!" the alarmed Oracle protested, whereupon Alexander immediately released her, handed over a donation, and left. He had heard all he needed to hear.

Some historians believe that this tussle never happened and that the story was invented much later by Romans bent on denigrating Alexander to elevate their own heroes. But either it really did occur, or

Alexander took pains to foster the belief that it did. Invincibility became one of his favorite themes. At the very least, it boosted the army's morale to believe the gods had destined its leader to be unbeatable. Moreover, it strengthened the connection between Alexander and the only other individual ever to be known as invincible theretofore: Heracles, the presumed ancestor of the Argead kings. The linked themes of invincibility, victory, and Heracles would persist as Alexander's career unfolded, becoming popular motifs on his coinage. ▨

Above: The ruins of a small shrine to Athena stand near the temple of Apollo at Delphi. The little *tholos,* a circular temple, was built early in the fourth century BC. The Delphic tradition of prophecy was old even then, stretching back to around 1400 BC.

Right: Nineteenth-century artist John William Godward envisioned this fetching Pre-Raphaelite Pythia. Modern geologists speculate that the seer's powers may have been attributable to hallucinogenic hydrocarbon gas. Ethylene, which rises from two ground faults beneath the oracle's shrine and also collects in a nearby spring, can produce a euphoric, trancelike state.

Above: Today, Byzantine ruins stand on a mountainside at Mystra, overlooking the site of ancient Sparta.

Above: An ivory plaque from the seventh century BC bears a relief of the god Anstaion, a minor deity associated with agriculture. Created in the style typical of Spartan ivory carving, the piece may have come from a Spartan temple to the goddess Artemis.

assemble at Corinth and conduct the legal niceties to make him official leader of what Philip had termed the Hellenic League. They scrambled to comply (Sparta, once again, excepted). Making his way back to Macedon, Alexander surely had no illusions about the Greeks' true sentiments. But he had bought time, and now he could turn his attention toward the northern tribes. Previous Argeads had done well to keep them at bay. Alexander, however, meant to gain some breathing room by pushing them back, all the way to the Danube River.

◆ • ◆

As a test, Aristotle had once asked Alexander how he would respond to a particular set of circumstances. He would not know, the boy replied, until the circumstances arose. The answer foreshadowed a key component of his matchless tactical genius: the uncanny ability to

grasp a foe's intentions and then adapt and improvise accordingly. His first display of this talent would come in the northern campaign that began in the spring of 335 BC.

During that campaign, in an early encounter with dissident Thracians, he found a crucial mountain pass blocked by a line of the tribesmen's wagons. It might logically be assumed that the carts were a barricade, but Alexander immediately saw that they were a weapon: Once he started uphill, the wagons would be sent rolling down to smash and scatter the phalanx in preparation for a broadsword charge. He told his men what to expect and instructed them accordingly. If there was room, they were to part ranks and let the wagons through. If not, they were to lie down close together, shields over their heads, forming a sort of carapace to deflect the carts. Using the second stratagem, the troops withstood the assault without losing a man, and the ensuing battle was a rout.

Later, in an ill-considered attempt to besiege the Illyrian fortress town of Pelium, Alexander found himself cut off by a relief army that had moved into the mountains behind him. To extricate himself, he devised one of the most bizarre (and brilliant) ploys in military history. Under the wondering eyes of the enemy, he assembled his men and put them through a long, intricate close-order drill. Back and forth several thousand of them marched, their terrible sarissas swinging left and right, up and down—in total silence. Then, on the king's signal, they began pounding on their shields and letting forth the blood-curdling Macedonian war cry: *Ailalalala*! Startled and confused, the tribesmen fled, regrouping too late to stop the escape. Again, not a single Macedonian soldier was lost, and within a week Alexander engineered a surprise attack on the enemy camp that resulted in a massacre.

And so the campaign went, from victory to victory, with the end result that Macedon's borders were indeed extended to the Danube. The hostile tribes had either been annihilated or were sufficiently cowed to stay quiet for the foreseeable future. All this had been accomplished in less than six months.

But the news reaching Alexander from Macedon was not good. Greece was once again a tinderbox, with Athens and Thebes fanning the sparks. In Athens, Demosthenes was spreading the tale that Alexander and his entire force had been killed in battle in the north—a spur to rebellion for restive Greeks who wanted their autonomy back. Thebes revolted, murdering the two top officers of the Macedonian garrison, and rumors abounded

Above: A ferry travels up the modern Danube, a river that once marked the northwestern boundary of Alexander's conquests.

Left: A Roman copy of a third-century BC statue of Demosthenes

Previous spread: Columns carved in the form of beautiful maidens adorn the famous Porch of the Caryatids on the Erechtheum in Athens. The Erechtheum, named for a mythical Athenian hero, stands near the Parthenon on the city's acropolis.

of a Theban coup intended to replace Alexander with his cousin Amyntas. Disgruntlement throughout the Greek peninsula threatened to coalesce into an anti-Macedonian alliance. Worst of all, Darius, Great King of Persia, was funneling in money to finance a general uprising. Alexander headed south with all speed, but not before sending messages to Macedon, including one for his mother: She was to eliminate Amyntas.

Amyntas's exact fate is unknown, but it is certain that his death came within ten months of Philip's, and it is probable that he was murdered with Olympias's connivance. She may also have gone well beyond her son's directive: By some accounts, she made Philip's young wife Cleopatra watch while Olympias personally killed their infant daughter Europa and then forced Cleopatra to hang herself. Obviously, neither mother nor child represented any dynastic threat, and even Alexander was aghast at the brutal overkill—although considering the carnage he was about to personally oversee, his sensibilities cannot have been all that delicate.

Meanwhile, in an astonishing fifteen days, he marched his troops 270 miles from Illyria to Thebes, proving to all of Greece, and most pointedly to the startled Thebans, that he was very much alive. The king offered terms to spare the city, but the Thebans decided to fight. They did, and bravely, but the end result was wholesale slaughter. The city walls were breached, and some six thousand Thebans were killed and another thirty thousand—children, women, and old men among them—were captured to be sold into slavery. Thereafter, the city itself was obliterated; in September of 335 BC, great and ancient Thebes simply ceased to exist.

The grim example was not lost on the rest of Greece. No Greek state would dare resist the Macedonians anytime soon. Beneath compliance, however, Greek outrage at the fate of Thebes hardened into cold hatred of Alexander. Any chance of true cooperation between himself and the Greeks he ostensibly led was lost.

That would soon be a distant problem, however; Alexander was within months of leaving Macedon, and Greece, forever.

◆　◆　◆

In the spring of 334 BC, the king set out from Pella with his expeditionary force, marching eastward across Thrace toward the Hellespont. It was the beginning of what was still billed as a Panhellenic crusade to avenge Persian transgressions against the Greeks, although the irony of that fiction cannot have been lost on the king. He was leaving behind in Macedon a force of twelve thousand infantry and fifteen hundred cavalry to deal with any trouble from his Greek "allies." This army would be under the command of Antipater, whom Alexander had left to guard the home front.

Top: A detail of a mosaic floor from the royal palace at Pella illustrates how pebbles of different sizes were used to create the designs of the main expanse and the border.

Above: These amphorae were excavated at Pella. The large jars—which could hold up to forty-four gallons—were used to carry and hold many things, most often wine or oil.

THE THEBAN SURVIVORS

Ironically, the brutal massacre and mass enslavement at Thebes contained the seeds of several of Alexander's most benign legends, among them his reputation for chivalry toward women.

After the city was sacked, a number of Thebans were brought before him to be judged, including a general's widow accused of murdering a Macedonian officer. She gave the following account of the deed: The man had forced his way into her house, gotten drunk on her wine, raped her, and then tried to rob her. She cleverly told him that her gold and other valuables were hidden at the bottom of a dry well in her courtyard. The officer, evidently none too bright, crawled down into the well, whereupon the widow and her servants stoned him to death. The king spared her, then ordered his officers to make sure there were no more such assaults on women of "a noted house."

Alexander's army, like most, did its fair share of ravishing, though Alexander himself was never known to participate. He was always squeamish about rape; it was not unheard of for him to have his own soldiers executed for committing it. But the phrase "a noted house" is telling. While he found the violation of gentlewomen appalling, he was not so particular when it came to the common folk.

In any case, the widow was not the only Theban to receive the king's mercy. When he issued his order for general slaughter, priests were exempted, and temples and shrines were spared from destruction (thus enhancing Alexander's reputation for piety). Also pardoned were citizens who could prove that they had opposed the Theban rebellion and those with demonstrable ties of friendship with Macedon. The latter category included the family that had been Philip's host during his time as a hostage in the city. Finally, Alexander—purported lover of the arts—spared the lives and homes of descendants of the great poet Pindar.

Seldom in history has a general so adroitly wrested good publicity from carnage, but then Alexander was among the earliest leaders to understand and cultivate the uses of propaganda. When he set out for Asia he would take with him a writer and academic named Callisthenes, the nephew of Aristotle. Callisthenes' mission would be twofold: To play Homer to Alexander's Achilles by chronicling the king's exploits, but also to send glowing dispatches back to Greece, lauding Alexander's virtues and victories and minimizing any setbacks. ▨

Above: The seven gates of ancient Thebes were immortalized by the Athenian playwright Aeschylus in his play *The Seven Against Thebes,* which tells how champions opposed one another at each gate during a civil war between the two sons of King Oedipus. Pictured are the ruins of the Electra Gate.

Opposite: Alexander shows mercy to Timoclea, the widow accused of killing a Macedonian officer, in this seventeenth-century painting.

The expeditionary force itself was built around a nucleus of Macedonians—most of them veterans who had served under Philip—and tribal allies from the north, along with strong cavalry units from Thrace and Thessaly. Once he linked up with the 11,000-man advance force in Asia Minor, the king would command an army of nearly 50,000 troops, including about 6,100 cavalry. Of these, a mere 7,000 infantry and 600 horses would be from southern Greece, and their use would be mainly as hostages to keep the home front pacified. Alexander would never trust them in battle, and on the road ahead he would dispense with their services as soon as possible.

Yet at the great adventure's outset, Alexander's spirits surely soared above such mundane matters as factionalism and politics. He seemed less the hard-bitten general and more the youthful romantic, dreaming his Homeric dreams. At the port of Sestos he left his second-in-command, the indispensable Parmenio, to supervise the Hellespont crossing of his main body of troops while he himself set out on a sort of religious pilgrimage to Troy. With some six thousand men he rode to the southern tip of the Thracian Chersonese to sacrifice to the gods before leaving Europe. Then, loading his troops onto sixty ships, he sailed at last for Asia Minor.

Although he had little appreciation of naval warfare and had never even learned to swim, Alexander took the admiral's role for the short voyage across the Hellespont. Clad in full armor, he steered his flagship to the point where he believed the Homeric Greeks had disembarked in their ancient quest and then hurled a spear from his ship's prow onto the foreign sand, claiming Asia as a prize from the gods. He was the first to leap ashore. Then, after sacrificing once more, he led his band off toward Troy.

This was not, of course, the majestic Ilium of Homer, but rather a seedy little tourist trap of a Troy that had grown up on its site. Nevertheless, Alexander sacrificed at what the locals assured him were tombs of ancient Greek heroes. Afterward, he and his companion Hephaestion followed another tradition, laying wreaths on the tombs of Achilles and Patroclus and then running a foot race around the monuments, their bodies naked and gleaming with oil. During the sightseeing that ensued, Alexander sacrificed his armor in the temple of the war goddess Athena, taking in its stead a shield and armor said to date from the Trojan War.

His spirit fed, the new Achilles left the old, traveling north with his men to rejoin Parmenio and the main army near Abydos. Alexander was now in search of battle, and the sooner the better.

◆ ◆ ◆

Above: A detail from a red-figure scene on an ancient Greek krater shows Greek soldiers carrying out the destruction of Troy. A krater was a jar used for mixing wine and water.

Opposite: Alexander approaches the tomb of Achilles in this eighteenth-century painting by Hubert Robert. In fact, the tomb the king encountered was probably a good deal less grand than the one envisioned by the artist.

Like his father, Alexander was bad at managing money. Sale of the Theban captives had probably brought in enough to make good on back pay Philip had owed his troops, but the new king was still badly strapped for cash. His best hope was for a pitched battle that might yield plunder to help finance the war. Had the Persians only listened to good advice and exploited this weakness, they might have swatted the pesky gnat on the edge of their empire before he grew into a ravening giant.

The advice came from Memnon of Rhodes, one of the thousands of Greek mercenaries who served King Darius. (Ironically, many more Greeks fought against Alexander than ever fought with him; the Greek mercenaries were among the best and most loyal of Darius's troops.) Memnon was an excellent general who had put up a creditable fight against Parmenio's advance force before Alexander's arrival. He was also quite familiar with Macedonian tactics. He had once been Philip's guest in Macedon and, in fact, was probably present at the meeting where the nine-year-old Alexander had so impressed the Persian envoys. But tact was not Memnon's best point. When he met with three of the region's Persian satraps conferring on how to repel the invader, he counseled a scorched earth policy: The Persian infantry, he said bluntly, was hopelessly outclassed by the Macedonian phalanx, and a pitched battle would be disastrous. Better to starve him out of Asia and at the same time use the Persian navy—far superior to Alexander's and nearly three times as big—to mount an assault on Macedon itself. Alexander might have to turn back to defend his base.

Piqued by the slur on their infantry, the satraps rejected this sound strategy and decided to fight. Aware that Alexander would hasten to meet them on whatever terrain they chose, they assembled their forces on a smooth, rolling tract alongside the Granicus River, about forty miles east of Troy. They took up position on the east bank of the river, where it was swift-flowing and about sixty feet wide. The bank was steep, its bottom slippery with silt—a daunting prospect to an advancing army.

Above: Among Alexander's coinage was this gold stater bearing a profile of Athena. The coin was minted on Cyprus.

Below: Envoys bear gifts to the Great King in this detail from a frieze that once adorned an audience hall at the Persian ceremonial center of Persepolis. The procession of gift-bearers was part of an annual New Year's rite in which Achaemenid monarchs renewed and reaffirmed their kingship.

Opposite: Macedonians stand ready to do battle in this vivid detail from the Alexander Sarcophagus.

Previous spread: Columns dominate the ruins of the temple of Apollo at Delphi.

Below: Macedonians and Persians clash in the Battle of the Granicus. The artist of this sixteenth-century bas-relief is unknown.

Opposite: Spear raised, Alexander leads his men in battle against the Persians in this painting by seventeenth-century French artist Charles Le Brun.

The Persians would need this advantage, since numbers favored the Macedonians. Alexander had forty-three thousand of his superbly trained infantry and a little more than six thousand cavalry. The Persians were far better off in cavalry, with more than fifteen thousand, but this amounted to almost half their total force. Aristes, satrap of Hellespontine Phrygia and commander of the Persian forces, hoped that superior position and a judicious use of cavalry would see him through.

As expected, Alexander sped his army toward the Granicus as soon as his scouts gave him the enemy's location. He arrived in late afternoon, prepared to do battle immediately, but cooler heads counseled otherwise. Parmenio, for one, took a long look at the rushing river with its high, slick opposite bank and advised waiting until nightfall, finding a better place to ford, and attacking early the next day. Alexander argued, but finally had to concede the obvious.

The following dawn, the Macedonians began crossing the river downstream from the Persian position, and most of the troops were across before the alarm was sounded. After easily repelling a token cavalry charge, Alexander was able to form up his forces, the phalanx in the middle, flanked by cavalry on both sides. The young king, unmistakable in a fancy helmet with two white plumes, took up his place on the right at the head of the Companion Cavalry. On the left, Parmenio led the Thessalian and Thracian horsemen. The Persians shielded their infantry behind a solid line of cavalry stretching wide enough, they hoped, to outflank the Macedonians. Memnon and his mercenaries were opposite Alexander, who was the first to charge.

At the head of a wedge of horsemen, he feinted left, then headed into the Persian center. Soon after, a corps of Persian nobles led by Mithridates, Darius's son-in-law, countercharged into the midst of the Macedonian phalanx. Alexander turned and headed for Mithridates, who flung

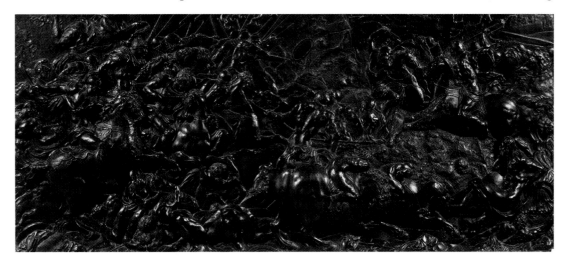

a javelin at him, piercing the king's shield and cuirass. Alexander pulled out the javelin and thrust his own spear into Mithridates's breastplate; when it broke off he shoved its butt end into his enemy's face. Wholly focused, Alexander failed to notice another horseman galloping toward him with battle-ax raised. This was Spithridates, the satrap of Ionia. Spithridates brought the ax down, cleaving through the king's helmet, stunning him and grazing his scalp. The ax was raised again to deliver the deathblow when suddenly both ax and arm disappeared. Cleitus, the brother of Alexander's childhood nurse, had saved the young king by slicing off the enemy's arm at the shoulder with one Herculean blow.

Alexander could hardly have asked for a more Homeric encounter, but at this point he lost a few moments, collapsing to the ground while his men rallied around him and held off attackers. By the time he could remount, his phalanx was well along toward polishing off the Persian infantry. Meanwhile, Parmenio's cavalry, which had been fighting a tough holding action on the left, made its own charge and the Persian line buckled.

It was all but over. Memnon and his mercenaries had retreated to a hill, where they sent a messenger to Alexander asking for quarter. He refused and headed straight for them. Ringed by cavalry and facing the phalanx, the mercenaries fought courageously, but more than half of them were killed and another two thousand were taken prisoner, soon to be sent to hard labor in Macedon. In later battles, the king would often hire defeated mercenaries. Here, he may well have decided that since he could not afford them, he might as well make an example of them. His rationale, in any case, was that Greeks who opposed Greeks deserved no mercy. Notably, Memnon himself had managed to escape, to fight again another day.

Thousands of his colleagues had fared less well. Some 2,500 Persian cavalrymen were dead. Infantry casualties were harder to gauge: Most of the foot soldiers had fled rather than fight. Aristes, the Persian commander, survived but soon killed himself, taking responsibility for the catastrophe. Alexander's losses were light.

The next day the king ordered the burial of the Persian dead and conducted elaborate funeral rites for his own men. He also announced that the families of the dead would be exempt from military service and taxes. It was a popular move, of course, exhibiting a generosity that would increase with time as he acquired much more to give. But his generosity— and his genius, his charm, and even his phenomenal courage—did not entirely explain the bond that was now forming between him and his army.

What mattered more on the day after the Granicus was that Alexander walked among his men, asking about their wounds, praising their valor, encouraging them to tell of their exploits, calling a great many of them by name. He made them feel valued, chosen, unique among men. For this, many must have felt bound to follow him to the ends of the earth—as they very nearly would.

Above: Lion skin frames this head of Alexander the Great in a Hellenistic cameo.

Opposite: Alexander exhorts his troops in this nineteenth-century drawing. Here the unknown artist seems to contrast the general's vibrant youth with the bearded maturity of some of his veterans.

Alexander knew he had to capitalize quickly on his victory at the Granicus. Away at the Persian capital of Susa, King Darius was now mindful that the Macedonians were not a nuisance but a real and growing threat, and he would muster his enormous resources accordingly. While he did, Alexander needed to translate his battlefield success into treasure and territory. To this end, he set out in earnest to "liberate" the western cities of Asia Minor.

Whether they cared to be liberated was, of course, irrelevant to him. Fortunately, it was often irrelevant to the cities as well. Persian rule lay lightly on the western satrapies: As long as they paid their taxes, they could keep their religion and customs and govern themselves locally however they liked. If Alexander proved similarly benign, then a Macedonian master was no worse than a Persian one—especially if the Macedonian was close at hand with a large and fearsome army backing him up. Alexander was surely aware of this, as his subsequent administrative policy would show. As long as he got what he wanted, the Asian cities could go back to business as usual. If they resisted, retribution would be swift, sure, and terrible.

Just after the battle, he made several moves that seemed to clarify his real intentions for the crusade. He appointed a Macedonian to replace Aristes as satrap of Hellespontine Phrygia. It was notable, and perhaps surprising to his Macedonians, that the Persian title was retained. He also declared amnesty for the Granicus survivors who had fled—merciful, certainly, but a bit puzzling in light of his ostensible mandate as a Panhellenic avenger. Now, too, Alexander began ridding himself of his "allied" Greek troops. Aside from the Thessalians, all but the contingent from Argos were left behind to garrison Phrygia.

Most significantly, the king instructed his army that there was to be no plundering of invaded territory, since it would soon belong to him. It was the first hint that he meant not only to conquer but to rule—an ambition far exceeding his supposed mission of liberation and vengeance. Did he mean to punish Darius or replace him as Great King of Persia? The question would linger and in time become momentous. For the time being, however, the amnesty and the no-plundering edict helped bolster his facade as a just and benevolent liberator.

Alexander dispatched Parmenio to take the Phrygian fortress of Dascylium, hardly a problem, since its Persian garrison had deserted. News of the Granicus was traveling fast. Certainly it had traveled to Sardis, where the king now headed. Sardis was a wealthy city, the capital of the satrapy of Lydia and an important outpost on the Persian Royal Road that facilitated travel and communications between Susa and the Aegean coast. As Alexander drew near, the Persian governor rode out to meet him to surrender both the city and its welcome treasury. In rich Lydia the king appointed not only a Macedonian satrap and military commander but also, shrewdly, a financial officer who reported directly to him. In

Above: Arches from an early Christian church stand before columns of a temple of Artemis in Sardis, Turkey. A virgin huntress in Greek mythology, Artemis was, oddly, also revered as a fertility goddess.

Opposite: Another view of the ruins of the temple of Artemis at Sardis. The cult of the goddess was very strong in ancient Asia Minor.

addition, Alexander took the opportunity to drop off some more baggage: Sardis would be garrisoned by the Argives, the last of his Greek troops, except for the Thessalians, and the new satrap of Lydia would be Asander, Parmenio's brother. It was a nice honor for the old man, and it loosened by just a notch Parmenio's hold on the army.

The king now moved to coastal Ephesus, the first Greek city on his route, at the same time dispatching two divisions of the army to accept the surrender of several towns in Ionia and Aeolia. In Ephesus he began an occasional practice of replacing oligarchies with democracies friendly to him (democracies played well back in Greece). Alexander also initiated the tactic, bringing Philip's old habits to mind, of playing local factions against each other to his benefit. In the vital matter of finances, he exempted cities under his sway from paying tribute to Persia. At the same time, however, he obliged them all to join the Hellenic League. As members, they had to pay "contributions" that roughly equaled the old Persian levies. Macedonian fiscal fortunes were looking up.

A pattern had been set, and it persisted as Alexander moved south along the Aegean coast, where he would face his first major opposition since the Granicus. Word reached him that the Persian armada was headed for the port city of Miletus, and he ordered his own fleet there at once. Arriving first, his ships were able to hold off the Persians while Alexander successfully besieged Miletus by land.

After this engagement, the king made a risky strategic decision: He paid off most of his fleet and sent it home. There was some logic in the move. His fleet was inferior both in numbers and skilled manpower. Besides, virtually all the ships had been grudgingly supplied by the Hellenic League. They were Greek ships, in short, and the League's captain-general probably felt that in a crisis they would desert him. To neutralize the Persian sea threat, Alexander declared he would close down all the enemy ports by land. It was an awesome goal: To reach it would require conquering or winning over cities stretching from the Aegean coast of Asia Minor, down and around the eastern rim of the Mediterranean all the way to Egypt.

As the Greeks sailed home, the Persian fleet headed a few miles south of Miletus to Halicarnassus, a large port city and capital of Caria. This was also Alexander's next target. Long ruled by

Above: The ruins of the temple of Artemis in Ephesus, Turkey

Below: A nineteenth-century illustration of an Athenian trireme, the most common warship of Alexander's time

Above: Sports fans in Asia Minor once watched foot races, wrestling bouts, and other athletic contests at this stadium in ancient Caria.

local monarchs acting as satraps, Caria had recently come under the control of a Persian governor. But its rightful ruler, Queen Ada, still held out at the inland fortress of Alinda. As Alexander crossed into Caria, he found the queen waiting at the border with a generous proposition: If he would restore her to the throne, she would adopt him as her son and heir. He readily agreed to this windfall, and the two soon became close. A widow, aging and childless, the queen delighted in pampering the courtly young king who charmingly called her "Mother." As for Alexander, he was assured of controlling Caria for some time to come, provided he could take Halicarnassus.

This would prove a much tougher proposition than Miletus, in large part because the defense of Halicarnassus was under the direction of Memnon of Rhodes, the brilliant mercenary general who had escaped the debacle at the Granicus. In addition, the city's fortifications were daunting, and it was well provisioned and could be resupplied by the Persian fleet, which

THE GORDION KNOT

How did Alexander loose the famed Gordion Knot?

Right: Alexander prepares to slice through the Gordion Knot in this detail from a sixteenth-century Perino del Vaga fresco in Rome.

The mystical and the pragmatic seemed always to coexist in Alexander's career; thus, though his journey to Gordium had strategic reasons, it is remembered best for his encounter with the magical Gordion Knot.

According to local legend, more than four centuries earlier a people had migrated from Macedon to Phrygia, perhaps among them Gordius, who gave the city its name and sired a Phrygian king, Midas. On his accession, Midas dedicated a wagon to a native god he identified with Zeus. The wagon's unique peculiarity was the knot that bound its yoke and pole—an immensely complex affair made up of many tough thongs of cornel bark, the ends invisibly tucked away. A prophecy went with it: The man who contrived to undo it would become lord of all Asia.

In Alexander's day the wagon still remained, near the temple of Zeus on Gordium's acropolis, and it was unthinkable that the king should leave the city without testing the knot. Shortly before his departure, therefore, Alexander made his way to the wagon, followed by a large and expectant crowd. Tension mounted as he probed and tugged at the tangle for some time with no result. Failure would be dire, bad for his reputation and for his army's morale. He had to do something.

Finally, shouting, "What difference does it make how I loose it?" he drew his sword and slashed the knot open with a single stoke.

Alexander's personal seer, Aristander, reported a different version, one that perhaps seemed to him to confer more legitimacy: that the king released the knot by drawing out the dowel peg that ran through pole, yoke, and knot. But the first and far more famous account is probably the right one, squaring nicely with Alexander's characteristic dramatic flair.

In any case, the Gordion Knot was indeed undone. And the prophecy would be fulfilled, but that lay in the future. Most likely at the time—a crucial juncture when Alexander had to decide whether to turn back toward Macedon or press on—the incident chiefly bolstered his resolve to continue toward Asia. ▨

Alexander was now helpless to oppose. In any event, the siege was long and the fighting savage. The Macedonians suffered many casualties, but so, too, did Memnon. In the end he decided to withdraw, but before leaving he loaded the Persian ships with all the personnel, provisions, and citizens they could hold, then set fire to the city.

Halicarnassus, or whatever was left of it, fell to Alexander. It had been a costly victory, but at least he was able to return Caria to Queen Ada. Leaving a contingent of troops to help her mop up Persian resistance, he bid good-bye to his adoptive mother and prepared to move on.

◆　◆　◆

With winter coming on, Alexander now reordered his army. Young soldiers who had married shortly before the expedition began were given leave to go home to their wives until spring. Also dispatched to the west were two officers entrusted with bringing back reinforcements from Macedon and Greece. The king sent Parmenio with a contingent of troops, most of the cavalry, and the siege equipment and baggage train back to Sardis, from where he would campaign against inland tribes. Traveling light, the king himself took his men southeast into Lycia and Pamphylia to continue closing down enemy ports. In the spring, everyone was to reunite at the Phrygian town of Gordium. This was a fairly central location and had some strategic importance as well. At Gordium the Royal Road running west from Susa dipped sharply south. Securing the town would interdict any enemy attack from the east.

Once they struck inland, Alexander and his men spent a hard, cold winter in uncharted mountainous terrain, fighting frequent skirmishes with local tribes. Heavily fortified towns were left alone, however, since the king lacked the manpower, equipment, provisions, or time to deal with them.

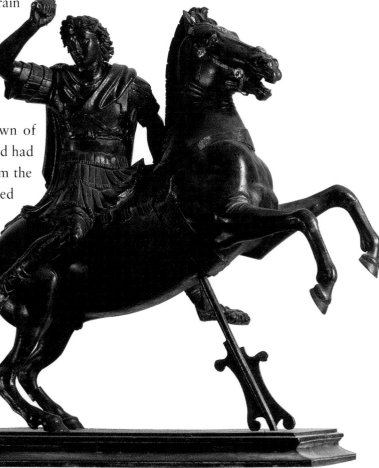

Above: A second-century BC bronze gilt head of Alexander

Opposite: Macedonians ride roughshod over Persians in this battle scene from the Alexander Sarcophagus.

Still, the winter could be counted a success; he acquired a number of new allies along the coast and inland, many of the towns and cities coming over to him voluntarily. By the early spring of 333 BC he was in Gordium, awaiting the reassembly of his army.

Within two months Parmenio's contingent had arrived, as had the men returning from leave and the reinforcements from home. The fresh troops—3,500 Macedonians, including 500 horses, along with a handful of Greeks—were most welcome, but the news his officers brought him was terrible. Alexander's old nemesis Memnon had been named supreme commander of the Persian forces in Asia Minor. He now had Darius's authority to implement the strategy he had proposed in the first place; that is, to use the navy to take the war to Macedon and the Greek mainland, and he was already pursuing that end to great effect. Some of Alexander's hard-won Asian coastal cities had changed hands again, and Memnon was systematically bringing the Aegean islands into the fold. Greek mainlanders were given to understand that he would soon disembark a large army at Euboea, and predictably, many Greeks were more than ready to rally to their fellow-Greek's side.

Alexander's choice was simple, clear-cut, and utterly crucial: He could turn back and try to protect what he had already won, or he could go on with his crusade. He decided to go on, even if it meant losing all he had gained thus far in Asia Minor, even if it meant losing Greece—even if it meant losing Macedon itself. He would always be irresistibly drawn toward whatever was over the next hill. To turn back simply was not in him.

And even as the king and his army marched northeast to Ancyra, where he received submission from the satrapies of Cappadocia and Paphlagonia, news arrived that must have reinforced Alexander's belief that the gods watched over him. Back to the west, while besieging the city of Mitylene, Memnon had fallen ill and died.

The gifted mercenary leader was literally irreplaceable, and with his loss Darius had to overhaul his entire strategy. With Greece teetering on the edge of revolt against the Macedonians, Darius nevertheless recalled most of his fleet from the Aegean, ending the threat to Alexander's rear. The Persian king needed every last man he could muster for what he now had in mind: a grand, decisive roll of the dice to repel the invader once and for all.

As Alexander turned south again and marched toward the Mediterranean, Darius, too, was on the move, traveling west from Susa to Babylon, there to begin assembling one of the largest armies the world had ever seen. Soon there would be another pitched battle, and Darius planned to make sure it was not another Granicus, with Persian forces outnumbered as well as outgeneraled. This time the Great King himself would act as general, backed up by the collective might of the world's most powerful empire. ◉

CHAPTER THREE

[AGE 23–25   YEAR 333–331 BC]

THE CONQUEROR

Above: In this bust, as in all his portraiture, Alexander is beardless. Though beards were fashionable in his father's day, the young king set a new style that persisted in most of the Greco-Roman world for centuries.

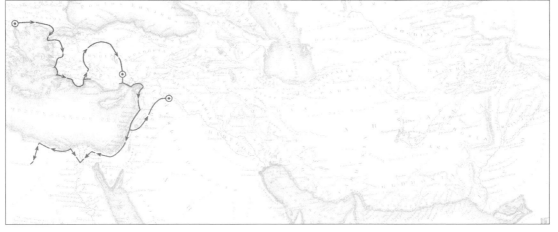

Above: The Persian monarch Darius I, whose long reign began in the sixth century BC, grants an audience in this detail from a relief adorning the palace treasury at Persepolis. The early Achaemenid king was also known as Darius the Great.

Opposite: The scene on a seventeenth-century Brussels tapestry shows comrades pulling a fainting Alexander from the river Cydnus. The king's plunge into the chilly stream almost cost him his life.

As always, Alexander was in a hurry. Leaving Gordium, he led his men on a forced march south across the bleak, rocky wilderness of Cappadocia toward the Cilician Gates, a narrow defile cutting through the Taurus Mountains. The Gates were poorly defended, and the army got through easily, still making good time through the sweltering, late-summer heat that baked the Cilician plain.

Their speed was a testament to their toughness, since they traveled with minimal food and water, and the barren land that made up most of their route offered little to supplement their scanty stores. By the time they reached the city of Tarsus near the Mediterranean they were tired, thirsty, hungry, and grimed with sweat and dust. The king, who shared every hardship with his men, was as hot and road-worn as

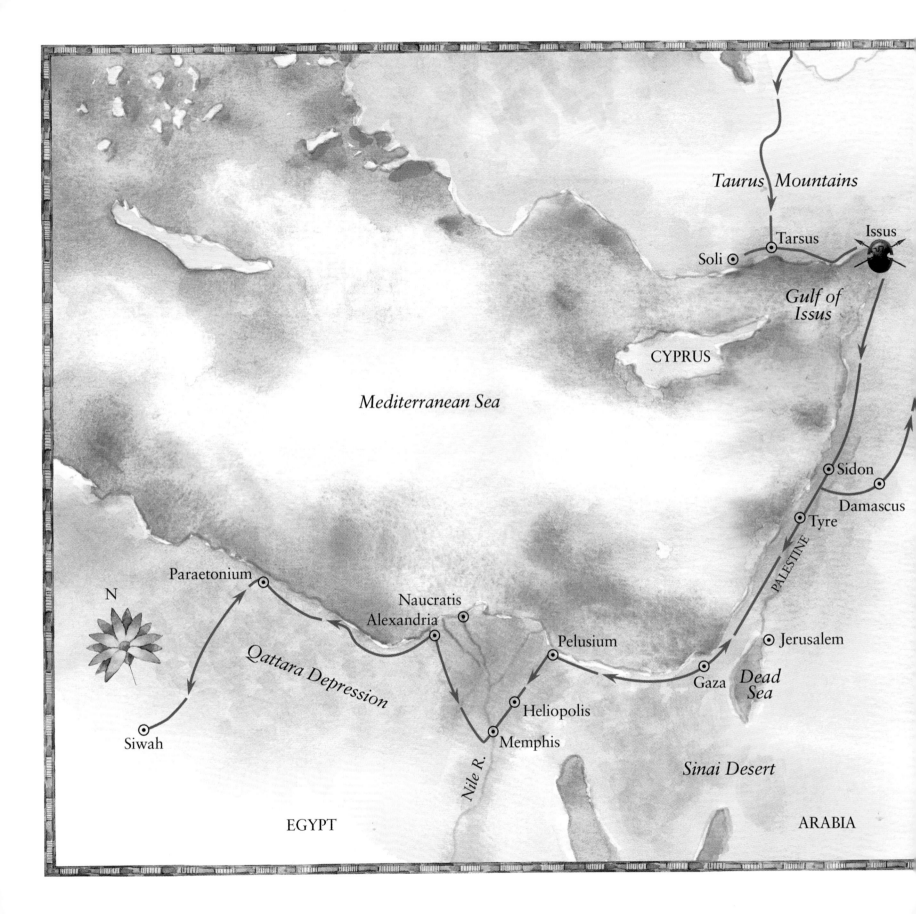

Taurus Mountains

Soli ⊙ Tarsus ⊙

Issus

Gulf of
Issus

CYPRUS

Mediterranean Sea

⊙ Sidon

⊙ Damascus

⊙ Tyre

PALESTINE

⊙ Jerusalem

Paraetonium ⊙

Naucratis ⊙
Alexandria ⊙

Pelusium ⊙

Gaza ⊙

Dead
Sea

Qattara Depression

N

Heliopolis ⊙

Memphis ⊙

Siwah ⊙

Nile R.

Sinai Desert

EGYPT

ARABIA

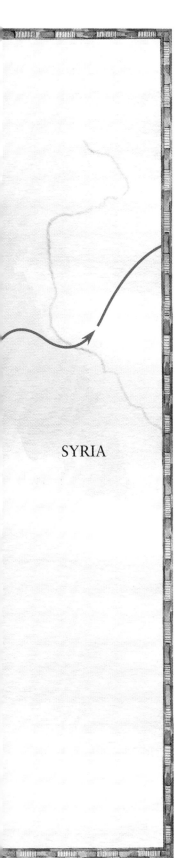

SYRIA

the rest, and just as happy to see the Cydnus River that flowed through Tarsus, its cold waters fed by mountain snows. Though he had been somewhat feverish and coughing of late, Alexander stripped off his filthy clothes at once and plunged into the stream.

The cramp that hit him instantly was so severe that his men had to drag him out of the river half-conscious, and within hours he was battling the onslaught of a fever that seemed severe enough to kill him. Most of the doctors in his retinue were reluctant to treat him, knowing their likely fate if he died. Fortunately, his personal physician, Philip of Acarnania, was braver than the rest. He told Alexander he could prepare a potion that might help, but it also posed a grave risk. The king told him to proceed.

Outside his tent his men waited, fear seeping through their ranks. They were battle-worn, in hostile territory far from home, their fate bound to the young king who sweated and shivered inside. If he died, all their futures would alter, and probably not for the better. Hours passed and anxiety mounted. With their general in mortal danger, it was probably just as well that they were unaware of what now lumbered toward them from the east.

◆　◆　◆

As Alexander had marched toward Tarsus, Darius had set out from Babylon with a host as resplendent as the Macedonians were weary and bedraggled.

First in this vast parade came silver altars bearing the Persians' Sacred Fire, followed by chanting priests and an array of handsome, purple-clad youths. These were followed by prancing white horses drawing the chariot of the great Persian god Ahura-Mazda, its drivers dressed in white and carrying whips of gold. Then marched the Immortal Guards, ten thousand strong, followed by weapons bearers and royal relatives who made way for Darius himself. The Great King—tall, slender, dark-haired, and bearded—wore a purple-bordered, white tunic beneath a flowing cloak embroidered with golden fighting hawks. His fluted crown was tied on with the royal diadem of white and blue cloth, and around his waist was a belt made of gold, holding a scimitar that rested in a scabbard carved from a single gem. His chariot, encrusted with gold and precious jewels, gleamed in the sun.

In its wake came horsemen and footmen attending the chariots of the queen and queen mother, their retinue preceding fifteen wagons drawn by mules and bearing the royal children, their governesses, and a number of eunuchs in their service. Last in the imperial train were 600 mules and 300 camels that carried imperial treasure, including the richly dressed royal concubines, 365 of them, one for every night of the year. Unlike Alexander, Darius decidedly did not travel light.

Above: On a sixth-century BC enameled brick panel excavated at Susa, sphinxes stand guard beneath a winged disc that represents the deity Ahura-Mazda. The ancient Persians, who regarded Ahura-Mazda as the one true god, were among history's earliest monotheists.

Opposite: Alexander traveled through the Tarsus Mountains and then waged the crucial Battle of Issus, fought near the border of modern Turkey and Syria. From there, he moved south through Middle Eastern lands that remain politically troubled today: modern Syria, Lebanon, Israel, Jordan, and Egypt.

Finally, stretching back as far as the eye could see, marched the imperial army: Persians, Medes, Greek mercenaries, North Africans, Armenians, Hyrcanians, and more, infantry and cavalry and charioteers, archers and slingers, surging slowly forward in what must have seemed an endless river. Some ancient historians estimated their number as high as four hundred thousand—an exaggeration, no doubt, but still the army's size was mind-boggling. Magnificent and huge, the host was also well fed and well watered, marching alongside canals through Assyria, headed west and then south toward Syria and the Mediterranean.

Meanwhile, in Tarsus the Macedonians waited, perhaps suspecting that the Persians were on the move, if not yet mindful of the enemy's exact location or its size. They would not necessarily have found its numbers overwhelming: Size did not always equal strength, and besides, Alexander's army had never been defeated.

Far more disquieting was the notion of facing the Persians without Alexander. All eyes drifted back time and again toward the king's tent, where their destiny lay in the hands of the gods.

◆　◆　◆

Soon after drinking his physician's potion, Alexander took a turn for the worse. His breathing became more labored, he lost his voice, and finally he slipped toward coma. Yet somehow he survived the crisis, and as the drink's salubrious effects took hold he began to rally. Within three days he was able to show himself to his relieved and cheering troops.

Still, his full convalescence took weeks. Not that he was idle (a state he always found intolerable), for there was much to do. Tarsus was secure—pro-Persian defenders had fled at his approach—so Alexander divided his army again. In a fairly short time he was well enough to lead one contingent in subduing pro-Persian factions in Cilicia. Parmenio, meantime, traveled east and then south along the coast. An oncoming army could reach the king's position only by crossing the Amanus Mountains through one of two passes, and Parmenio was to scout and secure both. This the old general did, first capturing a little harbor town to use as a base. It was located near Cilicia's border with Syria, where the Mediterranean curved sharply south. It was called Issus.

At the more southern of the mountain passes, the Syrian Gates, Parmenio learned that Darius's army had crossed the

Below: Alexander's physician, Philip, brings medicine to him in a seventeenth-century painting by Eustache Lesueur. Alexander apparently had total trust in his doctor. Legend holds that even as Philip arrived, the king received a note from Parmenio saying that the physician was being paid by the Persians to kill him. Alexander handed the note to Philip to read, meanwhile drinking the potion without question or comment.

Euphrates and was making its glittering, ponderous way west. He hastened north to establish an outpost at the second pass, the Amanic Gates, meanwhile sending a messenger to tell Alexander the news. It was now late October of 333 BC. By the time the king and his men marched east and rejoined Parmenio, there was more intelligence: Darius had pitched camp in an open plain east of the Syrian Gates, and he appeared likely to stay there, waiting for Alexander to come to him. The terrain favored Persian strength in cavalry. Parmenio counseled making a stand at Issus, where level ground was hemmed in by the sea on one side and the mountains on the other. There would be little maneuvering room, and the Persian advantage in numbers would matter less. But Alexander would have none of it. Convinced that the Persians would come through the Syrian Gates, he dropped off his sick and wounded at Issus and sped the army south.

For once he was wrong. On the other side of the mountains, Darius, who had lightened his load by sending his baggage train and many of his noncombatants off to Damascus, hurried north toward the Amanic Gates. Thus occurred the peculiar phenomenon of two large armies, separated by a mountain range, bypassing each other, each unaware of the other's presence. The upshot was that by the time Darius came through the northern pass and down into Issus, he was fifteen miles to Alexander's rear. Alexander was at the coastal town of Myriandrus, looking toward the Syrian Gates for an army that had vanished.

Below: A detail from the interior of a sixth-century BC red-figure cup shows a running Greek hoplite. The infantryman is weighed down by a heavy shield, spear, and helmet.

Darius now had the upper hand, with the option of marching south and falling on the Macedonians from the rear. But he failed to do so immediately, doubtless reasoning that there was plenty of time. At Issus he captured most of the Macedonian invalids and inflicted on them the gratuitous atrocity of cutting off their hands and then forcing them to review his army before releasing them to go tell Alexander what they had seen. A few had escaped, however, and they were already on their way by boat to inform their comrades of the Persians' location. As the news traveled, the Great King moved a little south of Issus and set up camp along the northerly bank of a small river called the Pinarus.

At Myriandrus, Alexander faced an unenviable prospect. His men had marched more than seventy miles in two days, and to aggravate their fatigue, a sudden deluge had left them drenched and shivering. Even so, there was little choice but to make them retrace their steps northward and, badly outnumbered, to mount a frontal assault on the Persians.

Alexander prefaced this unwelcome order with some stirring oratory, recalling past victories, praising the valor of individual warriors, and assuring the army that the gods favored its cause. In the end, the men responded with cheers and assurances that they were ready to follow wherever he led. By nightfall, having first had a hearty meal, they were moving north again, and by midnight they sought a few hours' rest in the Amanus foothills while Alexander went up into the mountains and sacrificed to the gods. At dawn they began the long descent toward Issus, and by midday they were nearing the enemy.

Alexander came on slowly, observing the Persian deployment as best he could. Darius had stationed a wide line of cavalry in front of the river to mask his dispositions on the other side. Concerned mainly with being outflanked, Alexander thinned his own infantry ranks to extend his front as the triangular wedge of flat terrain widened toward the river. The cavalry moved up on the flanks. At last the front stretched a little more than three miles, with the left flank against the ocean and the right stretching up into the foothills.

Scouts reported that some Persian troops had filtered into the hills in an effort to circle behind the Macedonian rear. Alexander sent his Agrianian archers and a few other crack commando troops to deal with the situation, which they easily did. Meantime, the king was still trying to assess Darius's battle plan. Then, the Persian horsemen acting as a screen suddenly wheeled and galloped back across the river to take up their final stations, and Alexander's view was unimpeded.

He saw that the center of the Persian line was the two-thousand-man Royal Bodyguard, seasoned and well-trained fighters. They were flanked by some thirty thousand Greek mercenaries, still the best of Darius's infantry. On the wings were Persian military cadets with archers stationed in front of them. The Great King himself stood in his chariot behind the Royal Bodyguard. Out of sight, well behind him, was his conscript infantry. Quite numerous but unlikely to be of much use against the Macedonians, these levies' main job was to stand in reserve and guard the tents of the Great King and his Persian nobles.

Alexander, positioned as always on the right at the head of the Companions, expected the brunt of the Persian mounted attack there. Consequently, he had moved in most of his other cavalry units, including the Thessalians, to bolster the Companions. This left Parmenio shorthanded on the left, with only the cavalry supplied by the Greek allies. With the

Opposite: Alarmed at Alexander's approach, King Darius is moments away from flight in this Roman mosaic depicting the Battle of Issus. The mosaic copied a Greek original that featured the most contemporary rendering of the battle.

Previous spread: Wildflowers tint a meadow alongside a grainfield in modern Syria. Olive groves cover the hillsides in the background.

Above: Macedonians surge toward Darius's chariot on the battlefield at Issus in this nineteenth-century pencil drawing.

Opposite: Jan Brueghel the Elder captures the tumult and carnage of the Battle of Issus in his seventeenth-century painting.

Macedonians still advancing, Darius spotted the weakness and began moving most of his horsemen, including his best units, toward the seashore to oppose Parmenio. Alexander had to counter by sending the Thessalians back to the left.

All this preliminary maneuvering took time, and by now it was late afternoon. Still Alexander appeared to be in no hurry, riding up and down his line, giving his men time to catch their breath after the day's long march. He was also hoping to goad the Persians into attacking, but Darius was no fool: He held a superior defensive position and was not about to give it up.

Finally, Alexander moved his front to within bowshot of the Persian archers. The sky instantly darkened with arrows, and as it did, the king and the Companions raised the Macedonian war cry and hurtled across the shallow river toward the enemy's left flank. So ferocious was the charge that the Persian archers scattered at once as Alexander and his men hacked their way through the light-armed infantry. Within moments, the battle on the right wing was decided. But elsewhere it was already clear that this would be no easy victory. The riverbank was as high as five feet in places, and Darius had it liberally studded with sharpened stakes. Struggling on this dangerous ground, the warriors of the phalanx were soon locked in hand-to-hand combat against the hated Greek mercenaries. Casualties were heavy on both sides; the river began to fill with bodies and run with blood. On the left, waves of Persian cavalry smashed into Parmenio and his horsemen, who had been ordered to keep close to the sea at all costs: If the Persians rolled up the left flank and circled in behind, all might be lost. They held their ground, but only barely.

Alexander, meanwhile, had turned the Companions toward the left, slicing through the back ranks of mercenaries and Royal Bodyguards toward the only target he really cared about: Darius. He was easy to spot, a towering figure in his gleaming chariot, but reaching him was another matter. All around him his Persians fought with demonic fury to defend him. Alexander himself was wounded in the thigh. Bodies began to mound around the chariot while the royal horses, panicked by the smell of death and their own multiple wounds, threatened to bolt. As Darius grabbed the reins himself to steady them, a fresh chariot clattered up at his rear, and he unceremoniously scurried into it and fled the field.

Alexander's every instinct was to give chase, but at this crucial moment a message reached him from the phalanx, still mired in the river and desperate for help. Parmenio's forces, too, were close to buckling. There was no choice but to go to their aid. Alexander wheeled the Companions around and charged back toward the river, soon clearing it of enemy infantry. Seeing their center give way and their Great King's speedy exit, the Persian

cavalry on the left broke off the assault on Parmenio and hurried east after Darius.

The chaotic endgame was at hand. Persian soldiers, horse and foot, scrambled to get away, the hapless conscript infantrymen scurrying desperately toward the mountains. Macedonian horsemen and archers followed in full pursuit, and the numbers of dead and dying littering the bloody plain of Issus mounted into the tens of thousands.

With twilight falling on the reeking field, Alexander and the Companions now set out after Darius, galloping twenty-five miles over paths clogged with fleeing Persian soldiers before finally giving up and turning back—but not without trophies. Taking to horseback (and at last traveling very light indeed), the Great King had left behind his magnificent chariot and all identifiable royal weapons and insignia.

Trophies were far more plentiful back at Issus, where the Macedonians were gleefully ransacking the rich Persian camp, seizing booty and inflicting on the royal concubines the fate usually accorded captive women. Excepted from plunder was the pavilion of Darius himself, along with his immediate family, which were reserved for Alexander. He arrived about midnight and settled into Darius's capacious bathtub to wash away the road grime before donning a kingly Persian robe and joining his friends to banquet off golden plates.

A discordant note in the celebration was the wailing coming from a nearby tent where Darius's family, believing him dead, was loudly mourning. Alexander thoughtfully sent a messenger with reassurance. Assuming on his arrival that they were about to be killed, the royal women threw themselves at the man's feet, begging leave to bury their king before their own execution. They were much relieved to hear that Darius was not dead and that they themselves—their persons, goods, and titles—would be treated with all respect.

The next morning Alexander, along with Hephaestion, made a personal visit to his royal prisoners. Darius's mother, Sisygambis, prostrated herself at the feet of Hephaestion, taking the taller and handsomer of the two men for the king. Told by an aide of her mistake, the Queen Mother was quite flustered before Alexander tactfully overrode her apologies. "Never mind, Mother," he said, "you didn't make a mistake. He, too, is Alexander." It was the beginning of an odd relationship, a closeness between Darius's mother and his greatest enemy that would last until Alexander's death.

Alexander also greeted Darius's wife, Stateira, said to be the most beautiful woman in all Asia, and complimented her on her six-year-old son. He then summoned the little prince to approach, and the boy, without fear, came and put his arms around Alexander's neck, presenting his face for a kiss. Much moved, Alexander remarked in an aside to Hephaestion that it was a pity the son showed more courage than the father.

Above: A woman standing at an altar is preserved in gold in this engraving on a Greek ring. The ring probably came from a tomb in Phokaia on the coast of modern Turkey.

Opposite: Women and children of the Persian royal family kneel before Alexander and Hephaestion after the Battle of Issus in this Charles Le Brun painting. As the king's extended hand suggests, he takes them all under his protection.

A FIRST TASTE OF LUXURY

On exploring Darius's tent after the Battle of Issus, a stunned Alexander remarked to his friends: "This, it would seem, is to be a king." Nothing in his background or experience had prepared him for what he found.

The royal pavilion was huge, and within it the stench of the battlefield gave way to the heavy perfume of spice and incense. In the torchlight, gold gleamed everywhere: golden plates and pitchers and bowls and caskets, all beautifully wrought, resting amid rich tapestries and fabrics. Settling himself into Darius's magnificent bathtub before dinner, Alexander must have pondered, perhaps for the first time, what the conquest of Persia would mean in terms of treasure. He was not a man who cared much for material possessions; even so, this small foretaste of unimaginable wealth must have been staggering.

And more was soon to come. Alexander dispatched Parmenio to Damascus to seize Darius's baggage train, and the old general, his mission accomplished, carefully cataloged his haul: Some 2,600 talents in coins—a year's revenue for Macedon, enough to pay off back debts to the army, as well as the soldiers' wages for the next six months—not to mention 500 pounds of unminted silver. Also: 7,000 pack animals, 329 female musicians, 306 chefs, 13 pastry chefs, 70 wine waiters, and 40 scent makers. As Parmenio packed up the trove and prepared to herd it back to Alexander's camp, he sent ahead two particular treasures that he deemed most exquisite and appropriate for the king.

The first was a bejeweled gold casket that Alexander admired enough to place within it his own most prized possession—one he always kept beneath his pillow—his copy of the *Iliad*. The second was called Barsine.

Barsine was a Persian noblewoman of royal blood, the daughter of the important satrap Artabazus and, remarkably, the widow of Alexander's worthiest opponent to date, Memnon of Rhodes. She and Alexander had known each other years before, she as a young girl and he a mere child, when Artabazus spent time as a guest-friend at Philip's court. Now in her thirties, she was beautiful, charming, and possessed of a fine Greek education. Alexander apparently agreed with Par-

Above: Exquisitely wrought by an unknown craftsman, this winged ibex once formed the handle of a Persian cup or jar. The Achaemenid-period piece was found in a tomb at Susa. Artifacts of similar richness and beauty must have abounded in the treasure acquired by Alexander at Issus.

Right: A silver bowl dating from the same period was once covered with applied gold figures. A few still remain.

Above: A fluted silver drinking horn, partially gilded, rests on a base formed by the head and torso of a griffin. The ancient Persian vessel was used both for drinking wine and pouring it.

Left: A solid gold pitcher features a handle capped by a lion's head. The piece is part of the Oxus treasure, the most significant collection of gold and silver artifacts to have survived from the time of the Achaemenid kings. The treasure is thought to have originally resided in a temple on the Oxus River in what is now the nation of Tadjikistan.

menio's assessment: She was exquisite and a pleasant companion, and with her he would form his first important romantic attachment to a woman. She would be his mistress for the next five years and would by some accounts (though most scholars doubt it) bear him his first child, a son named Heracles.

Alexander was not the only Macedonian to acquire a Persian mistress after Issus. Female servants and many of Darius's beautiful concubines ended up in the beds of his soldiers and officers and thus joined the Macedonian retinue. And, though the royal pavilion was off-limits, the soldiers found plunder aplenty elsewhere in the Persian camp: artifacts of gold and silver, jewel-encrusted swords, inlaid furniture, and valuable tapestries. One officer confiscated a royal purple carpet; another studded his boots with silver nails.

All this was a long way from the sheep pens and grain fields of Macedon, and if some of the soldiers longed for home and expected to return there after Issus, a golden cup or embroidered robe went far toward easing their disappointment. They had a foretaste now of the wealth of Asia, and it was a strong incentive to go on. ▨

Alexander's treatment of Darius's family was generous and chivalrous, to be sure. But like so many of his finer gestures, it was subject to another interpretation. He knew full well the importance of royal women in Persian dynastic matters, and the support of Sisygambis and Stateira could help legitimize his assumption of Darius's throne. The Achaemenid crown was now his unmistakable goal. Before Issus, the fiction of Alexander as crusader and avenger was perhaps tenable. But he was about to leave Cilicia, the last territory that could be in any way construed as a target of Hellenic liberation. From here on, he would be not a liberator but most emphatically a conqueror.

◆　◆　◆

As he had after the Granicus, Alexander visited his wounded and then buried his dead with splendid ceremony, but he wasted little time celebrating his great victory. Darius had been badly shaken, but he still lived and, Alexander knew, he could regroup. Several thousand of his Greek mercenaries had survived to form the core of a new army; and while the Great King had lost the best of his men at Issus, he still had his eastern satrapies to tap for more personnel. For the moment, Alexander was content to let him be, confident of the outcome of a final, decisive battle. Meanwhile, the Macedonians marched south into Syria to resume the strategy of closing ports to Persian ships. This was crucial territory, for the Phoenician coastal cities, along with the nearby island of Cyprus, had provided the ships and manpower that were the heart of Darius's navy. Fortunately for Alexander, news of Issus had paved his way; early in his march the cities fell to him without a fight.

Darius, too, appeared eager to avoid further combat if he could and to be left alone to salvage what was left of his empire. Alexander was accepting surrender from the port city of Maranthus when heralds arrived from the Great King offering terms of peace—most generous terms. He proposed to ransom his family to the awesome tune of ten thousand talents and to cede to Alexander, in return for peace and an alliance, "the territories and cities of Asia west of the Halys River." This was, in fact, all the land that Philip had aspired to in the crusade he had originally planned. But it was not enough for his son, who now crafted a remarkably high-handed reply.

Darius should approach him not as an equal but as a suppliant, he said, for he was now king of all Asia. "Everything you possess is now mine; so, if you should want anything, let me know in the proper terms, or I shall take steps to deal with you as a criminal," Alexander wrote. "If, on the other hand, you wish to dispute the throne, stand and fight for it and do not run away. Wherever you may hide yourself, be sure I shall seek you out." It was a response calculated to shame and enrage the Great King and to provoke the showdown that Alexander clearly craved as fervently as Darius wished to avoid it.

With that, the Macedonians moved south again toward the important port of Sidon, which pledged friendship. But the next target, the ancient and heavily fortified city of Tyre, would prove quite a different matter.

◆ ◆ ◆

Tyre, the most significant naval and commercial port on the Phoenician coast, was really two cities, Old Tyre on the mainland and the more important New Tyre on a small island. The two were divided by a half-mile of windswept sea, shallow along the shore, deeper toward the center. Above the sea, the walls of New Tyre soared 150 feet high. The city was a bastion that seemed all but impregnable, and certainly impervious to a would-be attacker who had no fleet. This was the sort of challenge Alexander loved—the chance to dare the impossible—and it was here that he would prove that he was not only a uniquely gifted field general, but also a master of siegecraft the likes of which the world had never seen. The siege of Tyre would be the longest, most difficult campaign of his career to date, and he would pursue it with dash, ingenuity, and a bulldog tenacity that no hardship or setback could shake.

He would not have done it at all, of course, if Tyre had accepted his offer to cast her lot with him. But the Tyrians, hoping to remain neutral, said he would be welcome in the old city but not the new. Irked, Alexander nevertheless sent two heralds with a final offer of alliance, hoping to avoid a long and costly siege. Violating a venerable canon of ancient warfare, the Tyrians killed the messengers and threw their bodies from the walls. Alexander's response was to begin dismantling Old Tyre to salvage its stones and timbers for building material. Unable to reach the island fortress by sea, he had decided to build a mole across its waters and thus assault it by land.

The Tyrians at first regarded the mammoth undertaking as a joke, but still the mole inched forward, propelled by thousands of man-hours of labor, both at the scene and by the soldiers away who were hacking timber from Lebanese forests. Increasingly alarmed, the Tyrians dispatched ships to either side of the construction site to harry the workers with archers and slingers. Many of the builders were killed. To counter the assault, Alexander had

Top: The ruins of an ancient stadium with tiered seating still stand in modern Tyre. The city is now part of the nation of Lebanon.

Above: This remnant of a delicate design in an ancient mosaic floor from Phoenician Tyre is a small reminder of a long and fabled past.

Above: An illustration from the *Histoire du Grand Alexandre* depicts the siege of Tyre. The flawed perspective, common in medieval art, belies how thoroughly the city's towering walls dwarfed the men trying to breach them.

his carpenters build two enormous, wheeled towers that were placed at the end of the mole. Inside them, bowmen and light catapults, shielded by leather screens, rained down arrows and stones on the ships. Tyre countered by rigging up a fireship that succeeded in igniting the towers. The blaze, backed up by Tyrian arrows and artillery, left the mole covered with corpses. Alexander stubbornly ordered that new towers be built and the mole's width be extended to two hundred feet.

Even so, he was beginning to realize that he would never take the city without ships, so he set off with a few troops toward Sidon, hoping to acquire them there. The results exceeded his wildest hopes: Several Phoenician cities, along with Cyprus, came over to his side, depriving Darius of the core of his navy and providing Alexander with a fleet of more than two hundred vessels, three times as large as the Tyrian fleet. While the ships were being fitted out with siege artillery, Alexander and his troops made a quick excursion into Lebanon to deal with forest tribesmen who had been interfering with his timber harvesting. The mission was successfully concluded in about ten days, and the king returned to Sidon to find more good news: Some four thousand Greek mercenaries, figuring that after Issus Alexander could well afford them, arrived to offer their services.

With his new ships, Alexander was able to bottle up the Tyrian fleet, finish the mole, and mount a saturation barrage by both land and sea. Inevitably, the walls of Tyre were eventually breached. Driven to extremity, the Tyrians defended their city with fierce courage but to no avail. In the end, Tyre met the same fate as Thebes a few years earlier. Seven thousand of its citizens were killed, another thirty thousand sold into slavery, and the city itself was left a reeking ruin.

As for the mole, that masterpiece of ancient engineering, it became silted up over the centuries, and in modern times paved over and then built on. It remains to this day, the core of a narrow isthmus still linking island to mainland.

◆　◆　◆

The siege of Tyre had taken nearly eight exhausting months, but the effort proved worth it. Now nearly every city of consequence near the coast, including ports stretching from Tyre all the way to Egypt, pledged allegiance to Alexander. The lone exception was Gaza. Situated on a hill between the sea and the desert, it stood astride the approach to Egypt. Gaza was the western terminus of the ancient caravan route that brought spice from the east, and the spice trade had made the city rich. Some of that wealth was now expended to hire Arab mercenaries to help defend against Alexander. Well armed and provisioned behind their tall, strong walls, the Gazans felt secure.

Alexander was equally confident as he marched the army south, having first sent Hephaestion on ahead with the fleet and the siege equipment: If Tyre fell, surely no city could withstand him. Nevertheless, Gaza turned out to be a very tough proposition. The siege towers proved all but useless, sinking deep into the sand surrounding the city. In addition, skirmishes with defending raiders were frequent and bloody. Alexander himself suffered a serious arrow wound in the shoulder, but, characteristically impatient with physical limitations, he ignored the pain and set about pulling off another engineering miracle. He had his men build a wall of earth and sand completely encircling the city and as high as the hill on which it stood. His heavy catapults were then pulled up ramps to the top, from there to launch a barrage from all sides.

Soon the city walls began to give way, and after savage fighting, Gaza fell. During the final action Alexander was wounded again, this time by an artillery stone that smashed into his leg and broke it. Still he pressed on, for now the road lay open to the richest plum of the ancient world: Egypt.

◆　◆　◆

Alexander's half-year sojourn in Egypt would change his life. In this timeless, magical place he would apparently confirm at last his sense of who and what he was and where his destiny lay.

Opposite: A sense of timelessness pervades this painting of nineteenth-century Tyre, as seen from the isthmus that formed on the remains of the mole built by Alexander's army. The artist was Scottish-born David Roberts, the great Victorian painter who worked from sketches made during his extensive travels in the Middle East and Egypt.

Previous spread: The modern city of Tyre rises behind a ruined colonnade from ancient times.

Below: The goddess Isis nurses the infant Horus in this Egyptian bronze figure, found at Saqqara. Isis, her husband-brother, Osiris, and their child Horus formed an important trinity in the religion of ancient Egypt, representing, respectively, the divine mother, the king of the dead, and the living king.

Opposite: On his travels in Egypt, Alexander would have seen the Great Sphinx and the pyramid of the pharaoh Khafre at Giza. Although they were already ancient then, the Sphinx's face was probably intact.

Previous spread: Ruins from ancient Gaza dominate the foreground in this David Roberts painting.

Here, too, he would leave behind his most magnificent and enduring monument. As though to presage these wonders, he was welcomed into Egypt with open arms: Here, as nowhere else since he had left Macedon, he was truly hailed as a liberator.

While Persian overlords in most satrapies were tolerated to one degree or another, in Egypt they were hated. With few interludes, the land had been ruled by native pharaohs for nearly three thousand years until, some two centuries before Alexander's time, the Persians invaded, eager to acquire this cornucopia of the Mediterranean world. Stupidly, the conquerors had ensured problems from the outset by traducing the local religion, all-important to the Egyptians. Temples had been defiled, the powerful priesthood offended, and the vast and devout peasantry outraged. The upshot was that Egypt remained in an almost constant state of rebellion, simmering or flaring, that had to be suppressed. For some sixty years the country had even managed to regain and hold its autonomy before Persia yanked it forcibly back into the fold in 343 BC. At the time of Alexander's advent, therefore, the taste of freedom was still fresh and the awareness of new oppression bitter, and Egypt was more than ready to embrace this young Macedonian king as its deliverer. When, in October of 332 BC Alexander arrived at Pelusium, the easternmost fortress of Egypt, cheering crowds were there to greet him.

From Pelusium the army and the fleet made their way up the Nile to Memphis, the ancient capital of Lower Egypt, unopposed by the twenty-thousand-man Persian garrison. En route the Macedonians must have seen in the distance the Pyramids and the Sphinx—ancient even in their day, inspiring awe then as now—and sensed the enchantment that seemed to permeate the land. Surely the spell was inescapable in Memphis, where, with great ceremony, Alexander was crowned pharaoh. In his hands were placed the crook and flail, making him shepherd of his people, and on his head the double crown, as he was proclaimed the son of Ra and Osiris, beloved of Amun, Horus the Golden, mighty prince, King of Upper and Lower Egypt.

The pull on the mystical side of his nature can only be imagined, for to be pharaoh was to be more than king: In Greece one could be the son of a god and still be mortal, but in Egypt the pharaoh was god on earth, the living link between the celestial and the mundane. If Alexander aspired to divinity (and he almost certainly did, as Philip apparently had before him), Greece offered him no true context. Egypt did.

After his coronation, Alexander sacrificed to Egyptian gods, paying particular honor to Apis, a deity who took the form of a sacred bull.

ALEXANDER THE PIOUS

Religion was a major force in Alexander's life, perhaps because it offered him inspiration and comfort—certainly because it helped him define himself and his destiny.

From childhood he must have felt linked to the Olympian gods, not only because Olympias hinted he was the son of a god but also because all the Argeads, claiming descent from Zeus's son Heracles, considered themselves "Zeus-born." Descent from a god was not the same as being a god, of course—at least not in the Greek world—but by his early youth he probably con-sidered actual godhood to be a viable ambition. From Aristotle he likely learned about *areté*, the special virtue or excellence that is manifest in great men and denotes great kings. To display areté in abundance beyond even the kingly, Aristotle taught, left only the divine.

Philip had evidently believed it, and it cannot have seemed all that far-fetched: The gods were deemed to be omnipresent in human affairs, of course, but beyond that, they often seemed very human them-selves—and not even in the good sense. Stories about them amply demonstrated that they could be petty, vengeful, capricious, faithless, devious, lascivious, and worse. Immortal and all-powerful, they were neverthe-less comprehensible and accessible, not so distant that one might not join them.

Perhaps with this in mind, Alexander was for-ever thirsty for prophecies and auguries, eager to know

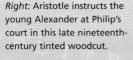

Right: Aristotle instructs the young Alexander at Philip's court in this late nineteenth-century tinted woodcut.

navy in the Aegean. But the mystical Alexander was nevertheless enormously pleased. Thereafter, he began dealing more gently with Greek delegations.

Along with seeking news from the gods, Alexander was faithful in approaching them personally. His sacrifices were lavish and amazingly frequent. On crossing from Europe to Asia Minor, for instance, he sacrificed before leaving, again in midchannel, and yet again on reaching the other shore. He took great care to determine the proper gods to appease in any place or circumstance; and along with special sacrifices, he was punctilious in performing daily sacrificial rites. Even when he was so ill that he had to be carried to the altar, the duty was never neglected.

Presumably on good terms with his own gods, Alexander had no problem accepting new ones that he encountered in his travels. Some he adopted whole, while with others he followed the Greek practice of syncretism, the combining of foreign gods with Greek ones they seemed to resemble. With only a few (if glaring) exceptions, he sought never to desecrate a shrine or temple or to otherwise show disrespect to any god, familiar to him or otherwise. It was his way to seek favor from all of them—and perhaps some sign of kinship as well. ▧

whether his deeds were sufficiently replete with areté to earn him everlasting renown on earth and a postmortem home on Olympus. He consulted his personal seer frequently, and he never lost a chance to seek out other oracles or search for portents: His visits to Delphi and Siwah and his encounter with the Gordion Knot are merely the most famous examples among many.

Good news on the mystical front could usually be counted on to improve his mood. While he was in Egypt, a delegation came to him from the city of Miletus with an amazing report about the oracle of Apollo at nearby Didyma. During the Persian Wars, the oracle had ceased to prophesy, and the sacred spring that marked the shrine had dried up. But with Alexander's coming, the envoys declared, the seer began to speak again and the holy waters resumed their flow. The practical Alexander knew full well that the Milesians were trying to get back on his good side, having collaborated of late with the Persian

Left: The oracle of Apollo at Didyma in modern-day Turkey was among the many soothsayers that Alexander consulted. Here are the ruins of Apollo's temple, where the oracle held forth.

Below: The Farnese Hercules is a Roman copy of a Greek statue attributed to the sculptor Lysippos. "Hercules" is the Latin form of Heracles, the semidivine hero who was the supposed progenitor of Macedon's Argead dynasty. Famed for his strength, Heracles is shown leaning on his massive club, which is draped with the skin of the Nemean lion, a fearsome beast he killed with his bare hands.

A Persian king had once personally stabbed an Apis bull to death and dined on its flesh, a sacrilege the Egyptians could scarcely bear, and they were now pleased to see their new pharaoh do the animal homage. He rose even higher in their esteem when he ordered the restoration of the great temples at Luxor and Karnak, which the Persians had all but destroyed.

In January of 331 BC Alexander traveled back down the Nile into the delta, this time along the westernmost of the river's several tributaries, the Canopic branch. Along this waterway, a few miles inland from the Mediterranean, lay the Greek trading town of Naucratis, a rather second-rate little port, but one that might possibly be expanded. (The flourishing maritime trade that had once flowed through Tyre would now have to go elsewhere, and Alexander may have wanted to divert it to Egypt.) Naucratis did not suit him, but not far away he found the perfect site.

It was a flat, narrow strip of land about fifteen miles west of the Canopic Nile at the edge of the delta. On its northern side the Mediterranean curved into the shoreline to form a fine natural harbor, a deep-water haven for commercial vessels and fighting ships alike, and to the south lay Lake Mareotis, a large fresh-water lagoon. The climate was wholesome and delightful, warmed by the African sun, cooled by sea breezes. Alexander had founded cities before, and would again, but none in so promising a place as this. Gathering his surveyors and city planners, he laid the city out himself, pacing quickly to and fro in his characteristic half-trot, marking where a marketplace should stand or a temple or theater rise in this, his new Alexandria. In time he ran out of chalk, so he ordered that ground barley be brought to him from the soldiers' mess to use as a substitute. He clutched it in handfuls, dribbling it across the ground, and it worked well enough; but it soon attracted flocks of gulls and other birds that gobbled it up as fast as he let it drop.

Alexander feared this was a bad omen, but his personal seer, Aristander, obliging as usual, assured him it was nothing of the kind. The birds' coming was most auspicious, the soothsayer said, a sign that this Alexandria would be great and prosperous, a city to nourish many strangers. And the prophecy would come true, possibly beyond even Alexander's dreams. Alexandria would be a magnificent gem among cities, the commercial and cultural hub of the world, the finest monument that any conqueror (or even any pharaoh) could wish for. Had he truly

Above: The Zeus-Ammon worshiped by the Greeks was later venerated by the Romans as Jupiter-Ammon, shown here in a carving from the first century AD.

Above: With a population of some twenty-three thousand, the mud-brick town of Siwah still nestles amid lush date palms and groves of olive trees in the Egyptian desert. Waters from the thousand or so springs that sustain the oasis are said to have medicinal properties.

been able to glimpse its future, Alexander would have been ecstatic, but for one small detail: Even as he laid it out, he doubtless walked across the spot where, in the not too distant future, his own tomb would stand.

◆   ◆   ◆

Founding a city was a religious act in itself, but as he pursued it Alexander was impelled toward another mystical venture, a visit to the famous oracle of Zeus-Ammon at the oasis of Siwah. This was no casual undertaking, for between the Nile delta and Siwah, far to the west near the Libyan border, stretched nearly four hundred miles, much of it trackless and unforgiving desert. Even so, Alexander was bent on going. Ammon, the ram-headed god, was the Libyan version of the Egyptian father-god Amun, widely accepted even in Greece as a form of Zeus. This god's oracle was a renowned truth-sayer, as venerated as the oracle at Delphi. At Siwah, Alexander hoped to resolve answers to questions that had long plagued him, questions about his godhood, his parentage, the ultimate outcome of his Asian campaign. He also wanted to ask about the future of Alexandria and, some said, about one matter in the past: Had the murder of Philip been adequately avenged?

So, taking with him only a handful of friends, Alexander set out, first traveling 170 miles along the coast to the Libyan border (there to accept a Libyan offer of alliance), then striking out toward the southwest into nearly two hundred miles of desert.

Here, too, enchantment lay thick around him. Early in the trek the travelers lost their way in a sandstorm and wandered for four days until their water ran out, only to be saved by rare and providential rain. They marched at night to offset the heat, sometimes through white expanses of sand, sometimes through defiles where cliffs and rock formations rose around them in fantastic shapes, and the broken shells they trod on glittered like diamonds in the moonlight. Legend holds that when again they became disoriented, magical crows and talking snakes restored them to the right path. At last a stretch of salt flats, glacially white, gave way to Siwah, lush and green with palms and fruit trees.

Below: After Alexander's visit to Siwah, coins were minted depicting him wearing the ram's horns of Zeus-Ammon. This one probably dates from the century after the king's death.

Alexander entered the sanctuary of the oracle alone, and he would never reveal what he asked or what answers were given. He wrote to his mother, saying he had something momentous to tell her alone when he returned to Macedon, but since he was never to return, even Olympias would never know what transpired. To his friends he would only say that he had gained his "heart's desire," but from that much can be inferred. It is surely no coincidence that after the pilgrimage the coins he minted often depicted him wearing the ram's horns of Zeus-Ammon, whom he now regarded as his father. It is also certain that what he heard at Siwah changed him. Afterward he became increasingly distant—as gods do—from mere mortals, more isolated and alone.

From Siwah he retraced his steps to the site of Alexandria, and from there he headed east again, soon to launch his army toward the heart of Persia, where Darius still waited. Whatever he had learned of his destiny, it now remained for him to fulfill it. ✸

CHAPTER FOUR

[AGE 25–26   YEAR 331–330 BC]

THE LEGEND

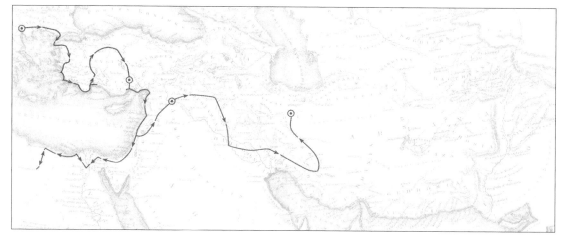

Above: Alexander appears as the sun god Helios on this fragment of a terra-cotta vase from ancient Greece.

Above: Alexander comforts the dying Darius in this sixteenth-century miniature. In fact, no such touching scene occurred. By the time Alexander finally overtook his fleeing enemy, the Persian king was already dead.

Opposite: An eighteenth-century, hand-colored copper engraving by A. M. Mallet shows the artist's concept of ancient Babylon. The city is divided by the Euphrates River.

AFTER ISSUS, WHILE ALEXANDER WAS TURNING SOUTH toward Tyre and Egypt in search of his future, Darius had fled east toward what was left of his own.

Barely allowing time for some remnants of his army to catch up with him after the battle, the Great King had covered the miles to Babylon with ignominious haste, entering the city with nothing of the splendor that had marked his leaving it. Back in his palace he was safe for the moment, but his prospects were dim and his options few. His army was shattered, his prestige tattered, and he expected that Alexander's army might arrive at Babylon's gates at any time. But in this—as at many crucial turns—he misjudged his enemy: Alexander had no intention of advancing eastward until Darius had time to recover from the shock of defeat

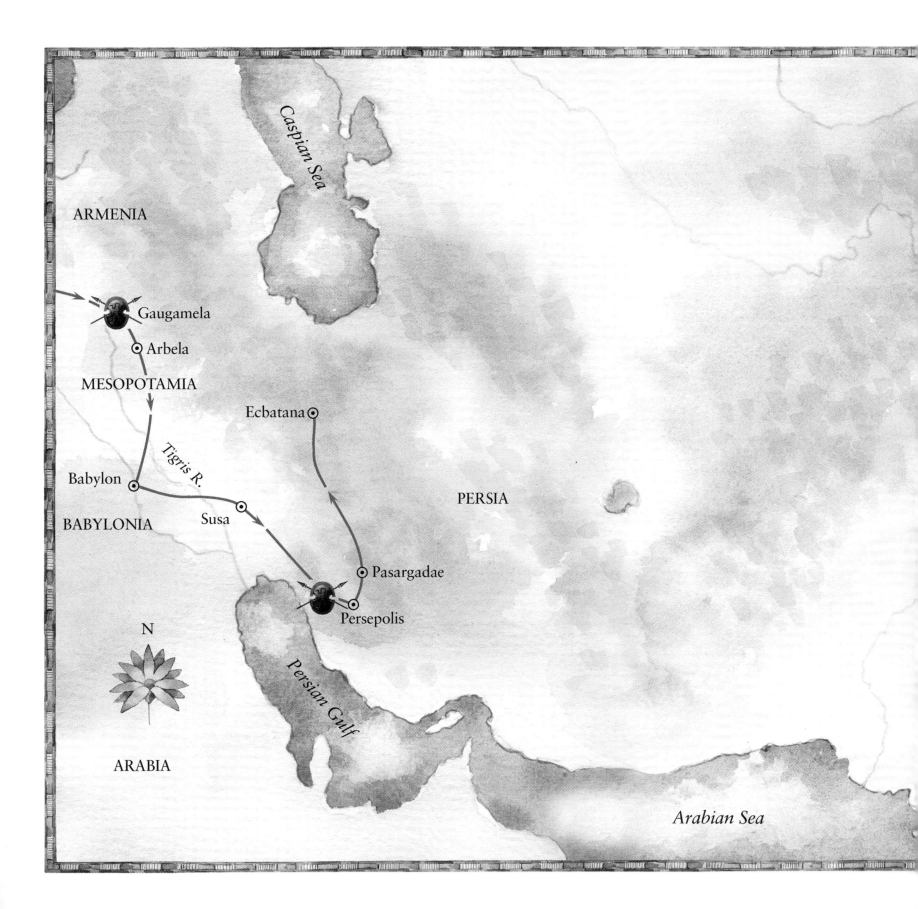

and to amass and field another army for a battle that would decide the mastery of Asia once and for all.

At first, however, the Great King had made little effort to assemble fresh forces. Instead, he initially relied on diplomacy, hoping that Alexander would not be able to resist his generous peace terms. The offer, of course, was disdainfully declined, so Darius once again resurrected the old plan of his late general Memnon: Use the navy to take the war to Greece and thus force Alexander to turn back. This was another misjudgment. Long since, at Gordium, Alexander had decided there would be no retreat.

Even so, Darius had pursued the strategy vigorously. Some of the Aegean seaboard cities, including Miletus and Halicarnassus, had already rejoined the Persian camp, and Darius dispatched many survivors of Issus to strengthen his navy, with an eye toward securing the islands and the other port cities and taking command of the Hellespont. He also mounted two other lines of attack. First, he directed troops to try to cut Alexander's slender line of communication through central Asia Minor; and second, he tried to capitalize on the ever-present discontent in southern Greece. An energetic Spartan king named Agis had been trying for months to organize a general revolt and had managed to amass a considerable force, taking over much of the large island of Crete. To help him, Darius turned to the greatest of his remaining assets, his nearly inexhaustible wealth. Money began flowing to Sparta.

But luck had continued to elude the Great King. Alexander's reconstituted fleet, bolstered by defections of some of Darius's best ships and crews, became stronger still as Greek vessels, in the wake of Issus, became easier to recruit. The allied fleet was therefore able to thwart Persian efforts in the Aegean at every turn. The Persian push to sever the Macedonian line of communication also failed. Alexander had left behind in Anatolia one of his veteran generals, Antigonus the One-Eyed, who fought and won three pitched battles to keep the way open.

Alexander, meanwhile, was well along toward breaching the walls of Tyre, a fact duly reported to Darius. With no good news from any front, the Great King had swallowed his pride once more and sent another, better, peace offer. This time he doubled the ransom for his family and offered Alexander virtually all of Asia Minor, along with the hand of his eldest daughter in marriage. Alexander's haughty

Opposite: This map marks the location of the Battle of Gaugamela, which opened Alexander's way to the richest of the Persian Empire's cities: Babylon, Susa, and Persepolis. Ancient Mesopotamia and Babylonia are part of modern-day Iraq.

Below: A limestone relief from the second century BC shows Alexander and Darius locked in battle.

reply was that he could marry the captive daughter if and when he chose, and he did not need the gift of territory he had already won for himself. Again the invader repeated his ultimatum: If Darius wanted to keep his empire, he would have to fight for it.

By now the Persian monarch could hardly have failed to recognize the truth of it. Indeed he would have to fight again, and he began to prepare. If there remained for him some glimmer that rebellion in Greece might save him, this wisp of hope was too shaky to lean on; Agis might be gaining ground, but most of Greece hated Sparta no less than Macedon. (Within months, in fact, King Agis would fall to Macedon's homeland army under Antipater.) So as Alexander finished off Tyre, conquered Gaza, and spent his enchanted half-year in Egypt, Darius reconstituted his army.

As the summer of 331 BC approached, Alexander, having returned from Egypt to the ruins of Tyre, prepared to strike eastward toward the battle that now inevitably awaited: He knew as well as Darius that the Great King's options had dwindled from few to one.

◆　◆　◆

Mesopotamia, Greek for "between the rivers," was the fertile seedbed of human history, immeasurably ancient. Bracketed by the Euphrates River on the west and the Tigris on the east, it had always been a fabled place, figuring in the rise and fall of empires, and for more than two centuries it had been the epicenter of Persian wealth and power. Now, with the approach of the Macedonians, it was about to endure another tectonic shift in human affairs.

In the broiling heat of midsummer, Alexander reached the town of Thapascus on the Euphrates, more than four hundred miles northwest of Babylon. The army crossed the river on two pontoon bridges, built by an advance party under Hephaestion. The crossing was closely observed by a strong contingent of Persian cavalry commanded by Mazaeus, satrap of Babylonia, but no opposition was offered. Mazaeus's directive was to retreat as the Macedonians advanced down the river's east bank, laying waste the land, for Darius was fairly certain that Alexander would take this route. It was the shortest way to Babylon, the gateway to the East and surely Alexander's destination.

In Babylon the Great King waited, having laid his plans. After Alexander had rejected his second diplomatic feeler, Darius had called on all his satraps to amass their military levies and join him in Babylon. Medes, Hyrcanians, Bactrians, Indians, Scythians, and many more answered the call, amounting to a force at least equal to the one at Issus, outnumbering the Macedonians more than five to one. This new army was better constituted and equipped than the last, very heavily weighted toward cavalry (Darius apparently had despaired of raising an

Above: Historic Baghdad, capital of modern Iraq, stands on the Tigris River. The ruins of ancient Babylon lie nearby.

Opposite: Today, as in ancient times, the waters of the Euphrates provide a lush but narrow border of vegetation that keeps the desert sands at bay.

infantry that could tackle the Macedonian phalanx), and bearing improved weapons—larger shields and heavy armor, along with swords and spears to replace javelins. In addition, Darius commissioned two hundred fearsome scythed chariots.

With this army, the Great King probably figured to meet Alexander on a broad plain sixty miles northwest of Babylon. The Macedonians would arrive exhausted, hungry, and wilting in the heat that daily rose above one hundred degrees—vulnerable to his fresh and well-armed forces. It was a nice plan, as long as Alexander took the direct route as expected. But Alexander, master of the unexpected, struck out to the northeast after crossing the Euphrates, heading across the Mesopotamian plain toward the Tigris, nearly three hundred miles away. This was higher ground, cooler, with bountiful grain supplies.

Forced to recalculate, Darius decided to hold the Macedonians at the Tigris, and he marched his army north. He had waited too long to set out, however, and in September, after a leisurely march, the Macedonians crossed the river unopposed at a ford where the Persian Royal Road met the river. About seventy-five miles southeast of the crossing, the road ran past a village called Gaugamela, where the Persian army now waited, preparing to make a stand. On an expansive field, the way was smoothed for Darius's chariots and horses, and stakes were lodged and ditches dug to slow an enemy cavalry attack.

Darius probably liked his numerical odds and the favorable terrain, but apparently he was not entirely confident, for now he sent a third and final peace offer to Alexander, who was

encamped about seven miles to the north. The proposal was staggering: all the land west of the Euphrates, a royal marriage, and thirty thousand talents in ransom money. When the king presented the offer to his war council, Parmenio, for one, thought it quite a bargain.

"If I were Alexander," the old general said, "I should accept this offer."

"So should I," Alexander rather snidely replied, "if I were Parmenio." He then sent his answer: Asia was not big enough for two kings.

Even Alexander, however, may have had a fleeting moment of doubt

Left: Brought forward into the Age of Chivalry, Alexander and his men take on the appearance of medieval knights in battle in this fourteenth-century illustration from *Romance of Alexander.*

Previous spread: Rendering the distance between the two rivers negligible, a medieval illustration shows Alexander and his army crossing the Tigris and Euphrates. The picture comes from Quintus Curtius's *Life of Alexander the Great* in its fifteenth-century French edition.

when, on the morning of September 29, he stood atop a hill overlooking the Persian encampment and got his first view of the enemy army—far larger and better armed than he had expected. The Persian cavalry formed a solid front wall numbering some 34,000 horsemen to Alexander's 7,250. With no sea or mountains to narrow the field, as at Issus, there was scarcely a question that he would be outflanked. He decided to postpone action until he could thoroughly assess the Persian deployment and the battlefield conditions.

Above: A Persian charioteer drives his horse in this fifth-century BC stone relief from Persepolis.

On the battle's eve he worked late into the night on his own plans. The Macedonians would be arrayed in their classic fashion, Alexander and the Companions on the right, Parmenio and the Thessalian cavalry on the left, the infantry in the middle, advancing at an angle. But to this Alexander added a new element. On either end, slanted back at about forty-five degrees, would be a strong wing of cavalry concealing interlarded infantry, and well to the rear of the front line would be an infantry phalanx held in reserve. If pressed, the wings and the rear guard could link with the front line to form a hollow rectangle facing out, able to fight on all sides. (Alexander was the first general in history to devise this formation, which would be much imitated in centuries to come.) The flank wings would also serve as a lure. Looking deceptively weak, the strong contingents of foot soldiers all but invisible, they might tempt the Persians into an ill-considered assault. Satisfied at last, Alexander fell into a deep sleep.

Dawn came, and still he slept. The troops breakfasted and waited, and still no Alexander. Finally, Parmenio went to the king's tent to rouse him, asking in consternation how Alexander could peacefully sleep as though the battle were already won. With a leisurely stretch, the king replied that he had been sleepless enough when forced to deal with Darius's scorched earth strategy, but now that there was a pitched battle, what was there to fear? "By Heracles," the king exclaimed, "he has done exactly what I wanted!"

With that, he rose, dressed, and began forming up his curious line of battle.

◆　◆　◆

Gaugamela, one of history's most decisive engagements, is also among the most difficult to reconstruct, for the simple reason that no one, whatever the vantage point, could have seen very much of it. It was fought on the dry, baking plain in a cloud of fine, orange dust, churned aloft by the scrambling feet of men and horses, and the wheels of hurtling chariots. Nevertheless, the recollections of survivors made the salient points clear enough.

The Macedonians made their oblique advance, luring the Persians toward the right. Soon the opponents were edging toward rough ground bordering the carefully prepared battlefield; further movement in that direction might hamper the Great King's cavalry and

scythed chariots. Thus Darius went on the offense, sending the left wing of his cavalry into a flank attack. Soon this Persian contingent, led by the Bactrian satrap Bessus, was fully engaged, and for a time the Macedonian horsemen on the right were holding off a force that outnumbered them ten to one.

At this point Darius launched his chariots at the Macedonian phalanx. The vehicles' wheels whirled with blades—but to little effect. Using the tactic Alexander had first devised against crude Thracian wagons in the Balkans four years earlier, the infantry merely parted ranks to let the chariots through, meantime hacking and spearing the horses and drivers from the sides.

The phalanx closed ranks again for fighting that now raged on all fronts, the Macedonians holding their ground as best they could against overwhelming numbers, slicing at men and horses alike. Then, amid all the clamor and dust, Alexander somehow spotted at last the opening he had been waiting for—a thinning toward the left of the Persian center. Forming every available horseman into the cavalry's characteristic wedge, and pulling along much of his infantry as well, he galloped for it, wagering everything on this charge.

It worked. The Great King's guard of personal cavalry and Greek mercenaries gave way, and Darius himself was exposed. Inexorably, the Macedonians began stabbing their way toward him. Then, nearly encircled, Darius somehow managed to extricate his chariot, wheel around, and escape. He must have known that this second display of cowardice would cost him his empire, but still he fled, once again deserting his army in the field.

And again Alexander was unable to pursue, forced to go to the aid of his hard-pressed left wing. His charge had opened a gap between the phalanx and Parmenio's cavalry, and Persian and Indian horsemen had poured through. These troops mounted the toughest resistance of the day before Alexander and his cavalry finally routed them.

By now the Persian line had buckled and was retreating, and Alexander was free to chase down Darius. Here the pattern of Issus repeated itself. As twilight fell, Alexander and a small retinue followed Darius's trail, headed toward the town of Arbela some forty miles away. By morning the Macedonians arrived there, but their quarry was gone.

This time it hardly mattered. The Great King might still live, but his claim to greatness was no longer tenable. The empire would never again rally behind a man so ignominiously and utterly defeated, not once but twice. Alexander, of course, could not yet be sure of this. Darius had fielded two enormous armies, and conceivably he might yet muster a third. Even so, when Alexander returned to Gaugamela to be hailed by his men as Lord of Asia, he did not turn aside from the salute. Who now was likely to withstand him?

In fact, at least one man might: Bessus, satrap of the powerful eastern province of Bactria. He had led the cavalry wing that ably fought the Companions at Gaugamela before breaking off to join the escaping Darius. The Great King might have preferred other company, for Bessus was an ambitious man, and he, no less than Darius, was of royal blood. For the moment, though, the two were merely companions in desperate flight, heading northeast with what remained of the army, toward the Achaemenid summer retreat at Ecbatana. The Macedonians, meanwhile, turned south toward Babylon to enjoy for a while the fruits of victory.

◆ ◆ ◆

In the celebration following Gaugamela, many of Alexander's veterans would have welcomed most an announcement from their king that their job was done. They had fought long and well and accomplished all they had set out to do; surely it was time to go home. The manifest evidence that Alexander had no intention of quitting left them disappointed and more than a little baffled. Obviously they were no longer liberators (liberating the Persians from the Persians?), and Alexander's declarations that he was pressing on with a war of vengeance rang hollow. He seemed more interested in collaborating and currying favor with important Persians than in punishing them. Was he still their Macedonian king, or did he truly mean to become the Lord of Asia, the new Great King of Persia? Even as the cheers of victory echoed, the seeds of resentment and suspicion took root. In time, they would flourish.

For the moment, though, Alexander salved the situation with lavish gifts to his officers and men, along with rest and recreation in a city uniquely qualified to provide them. Gleaming, broad-walled Babylon was renowned for its good wine, fine food, and gorgeous and obliging women. All these the Macedonians enjoyed—and all were freely given, for Alexander had struck a deal with his erstwhile enemy, the satrap Mazaeus. In return for a pledge of loyalty, Alexander had confirmed Mazaeus in his post, and it was the satrap himself who rode out with a colorful entourage to greet the conquerors and pave with flowers their triumphal entry through the blue and gold splendors of the Ishtar Gate. The visitors were

Top: The beautiful Ishtar Gate, named for the Babylonian fertility goddess, gave access to the Processional Way in ancient Babylon. Pictured is an exact reproduction of the Gate, built in Baghdad in the mid-twentieth century to serve as the entrance to the Iraqi Museum.

Opposite and Above: This smaller reconstruction of one of the walls that once lined Babylon's Processional Way was made of excavated glazed bricks from the original walls. It stands now in the Pergamon Museum in Berlin. Reliefs of sacred animals such as these magnificent lions adorned the ancient walls. A detail of one of the lion's heads is shown above.

Right: An engraved reconstruction of the Hanging Gardens of Babylon reflects the grandeur of the terraced complex of trees and palaces. The Gardens are believed to have been built in the seventh century BC by Babylon's King Nebuchadnezzar to cheer up his wife Amytis, who missed the forested mountains of her native Media. The cloud-shrouded ziggurat in the picture's background is probably the Tower of Babel of Old Testament fame.

Previous spread: A golden-helmeted Alexander makes his triumphal entry into Babylon in this seventeenth-century painting by Charles Le Brun.

treated to all the tourist sights, including the Hanging Gardens, a terraced wonder of forests famous throughout the world. And if the Macedonians were discomfited by their king's alliance with a Persian, there was enough drinking, dining, and sex to blunt the blow.

The idyll lasted a little over a month. Then, with autumn relieving the summer heat at last, the army marched southeast toward Susa, the empire's administrative capital. En route they rendezvoused with much-needed reinforcements from Greece and Macedon—fifteen thousand men, including fifteen hundred cavalry. Interestingly, Alexander assigned the new horsemen to squadrons without regard to the men's regional origins, and according to merit rather than noble blood. It was a small beginning to an effort that would in time become quite large: restructuring the army to discourage attachment to particular places or comrades and encourage the troops' loyalty to him alone.

Approaching Susa, Alexander was now entering the empire's heartland, and he would not get there without a fight. The way led through the lower reaches of the Zagros Mountains, and

Opposite: The rugged foothills of the Zagros Mountains confronted the Macedonians as Alexander marched from Babylon toward Susa. The army had faced worse landscapes, and would again, but the mountains were heavily defended and thus costly to traverse.

A ROYAL FAUX PAS

Alexander's personal charm was legendary, and among those most susceptible to it, apparently, were middle-aged women—not as potential lovers, but as surrogate mothers. The appeal he held for certain high-born women he chose to cultivate was compounded of several qualities: Doubtless his boyish good looks figured into the equation, but he could also be remarkably attentive and thoughtful when it suited him. And, there was the vulnerability of the ladies themselves.

Queen Ada of Caria, for instance, who adopted Alexander and made him her heir, had a sad history. Political expediency had landed her in a marriage with her own nephew (royal incest was common in the East; the Great King Darius's own wife, the beautiful Stateira, was also his half sister), and the groom was twenty years Ada's junior. The marriage was childless, and with the death of her young husband and her elder brother, Ada inherited the Carian throne. This might have seemed enviable, but it made her prey to a younger brother, who seized the crown and forced her into exile. She had known little familial affection, therefore, before Alexander entered her life. She delighted in pampering this courtly youth who called her "Mother," and Alexander returned her sentiments—perhaps genuinely, certainly because a kingdom came with them.

The stakes were even higher and the bond deeper with Sisygambis, Darius's mother. Alexander needed her backing to help legitimize his claim on the Persian throne, and she needed his good will for the very survival of herself and her family. When Alexander offered his assurances after the Battle of Issus that the royal family would be maintained in dignity and luxury, he won her heart. Even so, the gap between their cultures nearly scuttled the relationship in its early stages. After settling the royal family comfortably in Susa, Alexander presented Sisygambis with a lovely gift: lengths of fine, colored wool, along with some women who had helped weave it. The servants, he said, would teach her granddaughters to weave.

Hoping to please, Alexander was dismayed to see that Sisygambis was outraged. No Persian princess would ever do such menial work, and the queen mother believed she was being mocked for her diminished status. Alexander's assurances that his own sisters sometimes plied the loom did little to salve her feelings, and the king had to expend considerable time and all his formidable charm to mend the gaffe. ▧

there, at a crucial pass, he encountered savage Persian resistance and suffered heavy losses before winning his way through. There was recompense enough, however, once he reached the capital. There, another obliging satrap ceded him the city, including the royal palace and its treasury, a haul that even Alexander must have found unimaginable. There were between forty thousand and fifty thousand talents in unminted gold and silver, along with another nine thousand talents in gold coin, not to mention fabulous fabrics and other luxuries. The rest of the palace was a treasure in itself, floored in marble and malachite, filled with jewels and gold plate and marvelous works of art. But for a man whose main interest in money lay only in translating it into power, a greater pleasure was to come. Leaving the treasury, Alexander went directly to the royal reception hall and settled himself onto the golden Achaemenid throne, forbidden to any but a Great King.

Unfortunately, the grand gesture was marred by a rather comic circumstance. Darius was said to be six and a half feet tall. Alexander was at least a foot shorter, and his legs dangled childlike above the royal footstool. A horrified aide rushed to substitute one of Darius's tables, and on these Alexander's feet rested comfortably. A Persian eunuch was heard weeping at the desecration, but there the table stayed.

The Macedonians remained only briefly in Susa. Alexander left troops to protect the treasury, and he also left behind Darius's family, which had traveled with him all the way from Issus, settling them in palatial comfort and also providing a tutor to teach them Greek. Then he took to the road again, continuing southeast. His destination now was Persepolis, the lovely, ceremonial heart of the empire. Here he would show that whatever else he was—Hellenic avenger, Macedonian king, Lord of Asia—he was also still one thing more: a Balkan barbarian.

◆　◆　◆

Persepolis was not a city as such; rather, it was a caretaker town whose purpose was to serve and maintain an elaborate complex of palaces, erected on a vast, sixty-foot-high terrace. The Achaemenid kings were buried nearby, and it was at Persepolis that they stored their treasure—their personal wealth, as opposed to the governmental treasury at Susa. Persepolis was also the site of the most solemn of dynastic festivals, held each April on the Persian New Year. From all points of the far-flung empire emissaries would come, bearing tribute to be laid at the feet of the Great King in the hundred-columned Hall of Xerxes. This was also the occasion for the monarch to prove his mettle in ritual combat with evil demons, emerging triumphant with his kingship renewed and himself reaffirmed as the anointed one of the great god Ahura-Mazda. It was a holy place in this sense, and it was the living symbol of the dynastic continuity of the Achaemenids.

Above: This base of a ruined column once helped support the Achaemenid royal palace at Susa. Ancient Susa is now Shush, Iran.

Right: A doorjamb bearing a relief of the Great King Xerxes on his throne once stood in the Hall of One Hundred Columns at Persepolis.

Perhaps for this reason Alexander assured his troops that Persepolis was the most hateful city in Asia, and on entering it in January of 330 BC, he immediately loosed them to plunder it. The resulting orgy of murder, rape, pillage, and vandalism was so savage that the Macedonians took to killing each other over the spoils before the king finally called a halt to it. Exempted only were the palaces and their treasure; these were reserved for Alexander.

He stayed in Persepolis for more than four months. Intelligence reports informed him that to the north in Ecbatana, Darius was recruiting troops for a new army. But the intervening mountains were all but impassable in winter, so Alexander spent the time pacifying the rustic peoples of the province (a sport he always seemed to enjoy) and hunting in the more conventional sense. There was also the task of systematically looting the palaces of every last scrap and vestige of treasure.

The haul from Persepolis was staggering: at least seven million and perhaps as many as eleven million pounds of gold and silver, along with jewels, priceless rugs and tapestries, and precious artifacts. An enormous caravan had to be assembled to cart it all to Susa to join the governmental treasure. Eventually, the entire horde would be moved to Ecbatana.

With this massed fortune, as well as his previous conquests and his patrimony from Macedon, Alexander became the richest man in the world—the richest, in fact, who had ever lived. With his usual fiscal unconcern, he kept with him only enough to support the army. Even so, the almost infinite wealth would work on him in subtle ways, removing one of the few remaining restraints on his ravenous ambition. Now he could buy armies if he needed them, and bribe away dissent. The money left him more powerful than ever, and more alone.

As he whiled away the time in Persepolis, Alexander may have hoped as April approached that the New Year ceremony would be held as usual and that the Persian nobles and the Magi, the powerful priestly class, would recognize his strength and confirm him as the new Achaemenid king. This was not to be, of course, for the Magi especially regarded him as a godless, violent, uncouth usurper. So, as the spring thaws came and the mountain passes opened, he prepared to take his godless, violent, uncouth leave.

One night, perhaps during a drunken party, Alexander and his confederates torched the palaces. Fed by rich cedar beams and pillars, the conflagration consumed almost everything. If the Greeks wanted vengeance, Alexander had certainly delivered, for the sacred city of the Achaemenids was no more.

THE BURNING OF PERSEPOLIS

Why did Alexander torch the sacred center of the Persian Empire?

Alexander's destruction of Persepolis is among the most controversial acts of his career, not just because it was so barbaric, but because the motive behind it has always been in dispute. One tradition holds that it was a political act of vengeance, well reasoned and intentional. Another—more romantic and intriguing by far—involves wine, a whim, and a woman.

The latter legend holds that toward the end of his stay in Persepolis, Alexander held a feast in the hundred-columned Hall of Xerxes. Women were on hand at this particular party, among them a beautiful Athenian courtesan, Thais. She had traveled with the army all across Asia to be with her patron Ptolemy, one of Alexander's favorite generals.

As usual, the celebrants were well lubricated with wine, and songs provided by female musicians added to the festive mood. As the evening wore on, Thais rose and made a speech, teasing Alexander. His soldiers, she said, had punished Persia, and now it should be the women's turn to avenge the desecration of Athens. Would the king join her in a revel?

Sodden but still mobile, Alexander sprang to his feet, grabbed a torch, and called for a procession in honor of Dionysus. His guests seized torches of their own, and with Thais leading the way they danced giddily across the floor of the enormous hall. At last Alexander, then Thais, flung their torches, and the guests followed suit. Fabrics and furniture ignited at once, and the flames soon began licking upward along the sixty-foot-high columns to the cedar ceiling. In no time, the destruction was complete. The partygoers cheered merrily throughout this consummate act of vandalism, although Alexander, by some accounts, was filled with regret at his impulsive act once he sobered up.

Another version of the story suggests that the arson, far from being capricious, was coldly calculated by Alexander. By this account, the king discussed torching the palaces in advance. Parmenio advised him against it, arguing that it made no sense to destroy property that he now owned. Besides, the general said, the Persians would never accept him after such a desecration. Alexander was not dissuaded. He intended to avenge the Persians' invasion of Greece and their burning of the Athenian temples.

Given Alexander's customary pragmatism, this intentional torching seems more believable. Before Persepolis, the king had usually avoided offending Persian sensibilities, hoping that he would be accepted as Darius's successor. But as it became increasingly clear that this would never happen, he may have seen no reason to continue being conciliatory. If he could not inherit the Achaemenid mantle, then he might as well destroy Persepolis, the dynasty's ancestral heart. The gesture would make an indelible statement: What the Persians would not give him freely, he would take by force.

Also arguing for the second version is the timing: Alexander did not destroy the royal complex until every trace of treasure had been removed. What he burned was little more than an empty shell.

On the other hand, it is possible—even probable—to find some truth in both accounts. Ptolemy himself, the main source who asserted the burning was intentional, was a biographer who had several axes to grind. A few years older than Alexander, Ptolemy had been the king's lifelong friend. It was even rumored, though falsely, that the two were half brothers, Ptolemy being Philip's bastard by a precocious

relationship with Ptolemy's mother. Given their closeness, Ptolemy, writing long after Alexander's death, would not have wanted to impugn his old friend's memory by laying the charge of mindless vandalism at his door.

Neither would Ptolemy want to sully the name of his mistress Thais. Theirs was no casual affair, but apparently a long-term love match. She eventually bore him three children and remained with him throughout his own fascinating career, even after he had become a king himself, had married for political reasons, and had founded a powerful dynasty of his own. Even if Thais had been the seductive spark that ignited Persepolis, Ptolemy was hardly the man to recount the fact.

Finally, Ptolemy had a suspect political motive. He had been Parmenio's rival and was fond of portraying the old general as a cautious sycophant who forever gave advice that Alexander never heeded. The portrait was grossly unfair, but it fits perfectly into the scene—possibly fabricated—in which Alexander brushes aside Parmenio's call for restraint and proceeds with a noble act of vengeance.

The whole truth of what happened at Persepolis is probably beyond retrieval. It is not unreasonable to conclude, however, that in burning the palaces, Alexander simply capitalized on a suitably dramatic setting—of wine, music, and a beautiful woman—to do what he had meant to do anyway. ▨

Above: A relief of Persian and Median soldiers adorns a wall at Persepolis. The Medians, such as the one shown here in the center, are distinguished by their round headdresses. Ironically, the fire Alexander started hardened and thus helped preserve some of the priceless art at the Achaemenid citadel.

Left: Double volutes in the shape of bulls' heads formed the capital of a column at Persepolis.

But the flames that consumed Persepolis also devoured whatever chance existed for Alexander to be regarded as Darius's legitimate successor. Persian resistance to the invader would now stiffen and coalesce into a stubborn nationalism, and Alexander's best hope for truly becoming the Lord of Asia lay in finding Darius and forcing him to abdicate.

◆ ◆ ◆

Early in June, the army set out for Ecbatana, a journey of some five hundred miles north; but with only one hundred miles to go, Alexander learned that his quarry had eluded him again. Word reached him that Darius had failed to raise a new army and had therefore fled eastward again, skirting the southern coast of the Caspian Sea, apparently headed for the satrapy of Bactria. Bessus and the Bactrian cavalry were with him, along with six thousand foot soldiers and his die-hard Greek mercenaries. Alexander marched on to Ecbatana, but there he paused in the chase to make some changes in his own forces that would have far-reaching consequences.

Above: Armed in the style of the sixth century BC, Persian infantrymen march in this frieze that adorned the staircase in the Audience Hall of Darius the Great at Persepolis.

The Hellenic crusade was now unarguably over. The "liberating" of Greek cities in Asia Minor was long since complete, and the destruction of Persepolis was surely adequate revenge. Moreover, it appeared that Darius would offer no more pitched battles on the order of Issus or Gaugamela. Therefore, Alexander released all his Greek troops, including Parmenio's valiant Thessalian cavalry. Each man got a handsome bonus and godspeed for a good trip home—if that was what he wanted. On the other hand, each man who chose to reenlist was offered a bonus of three talents. However hungry for home, a great many found the inducement too good to pass up. The package cost Alexander upward of thirteen thousand talents, but he could certainly afford it, and what he got was a bargain at any price: a skilled and veteran mercenary army, loyal only to him, bound to follow wherever he led, with no pretense of crusades and causes.

At the same time, Alexander effectively got rid of Parmenio. It was tactfully done, of course. The old general was in his seventies now and due for some easy duty. He would be left behind with some twenty-five thousand troops and a temporary additional force of six thousand to oversee moving the treasure from Susa to Ecbatana and then to pacify territory south of the Caspian. There was no dishonor in it, but both king and general knew what the new assignment really meant: Parmenio's power was at an end. He may have been indispensable heretofore, but the relationship between him and Alexander had always been uneasy. Parmenio was a rival for the army's affections and—worse—he had been Philip's man, first and foremost, the living embodiment of the Old Guard. How often in his presence Alexander must have felt himself silently weighed, compared, judged. Now, at last, the king would be free of him.

Resuming his pursuit of Darius, Alexander pressed eastward in a midsummer heat so relentless that men and horses died along the way from dehydration. En route, the beleaguered column was overtaken by news of a shocking coup: Darius had been deposed by Bessus and by his own grand vizier, Nabarzanes. Bessus had declared himself Great King, and Darius was being held prisoner, a bargaining chip to be traded if the Macedonians came too close. Urging his flagging troops to even greater speed, Alexander mounted an all-night march that brought him to a village where he learned of a dangerous short cut through harsh desert. The king left behind all but five hundred men, his fittest troops, and set out, once again traveling through the night. At first light, he finally sighted the enemy.

Above: A mosque rises above Tehran University. The modern capital of Iran lies near the ancient site of Ecbatana, the summer retreat of Persia's Achaemenid kings.

Right: A Roman portrait bust of Alexander

The Persians were far superior numerically, and had they stood their ground they might have killed Alexander there and then. But, believing themselves at least two days ahead of him, they were so startled by his approach that their only thought was to flee, and the faster the better. First, however, they had to deal with their royal encumbrance. It would not do to let Alexander take Darius alive and perhaps use him to press his own claim to the throne.

For camouflage, Darius was being held in a common covered wagon, drawn by oxen. The conspirators begged him to mount a horse and ride with them, but the deposed monarch summoned all that remained of his dignity and refused. Better to beg mercy of Alexander, he said, than to travel any farther with traitors. In no mood to debate, Bessus and his confederates stabbed him with javelins and left him in the wagon. Then they divided their forces and set out at top speed, traveling in different directions.

With no idea which column to follow, the Macedonians were forced to halt. Frustrated, they examined the Persians' abandoned baggage train, hoping for some sign of Darius. But he was no longer there. His wagon's oxen, driverless and thirsty, had wandered off in search of water, coming to rest at a small spring about half a mile away from Alexander's men. He was found there by a Macedonian soldier named Polystratus who, looking for water himself, heard moaning from inside the wagon and went to investigate.

On the floor of the rude vehicle lay Darius, once master of much of the world, drenched in blood that pooled and flowed from around the javelins embedded in his chest, his only companion a dog that cringed at his side. Bending near, Polystratus heard a whispered request for water. He fetched some in his helmet and brought it to the dying man. Darius drank, then reached weakly for the soldier's hand and held it, saying he was grateful to heaven that he did not have to die alone. With that, he was gone.

Polystratus hurried to tell Alexander, who at once made his way to the wagon. Alexander gazed down at Darius, so diminished in death, perhaps pondering momentarily the fate of rulers, however great. Wordless, he stripped off his own cloak and gently wrapped it around the body. This was no enemy now, only a king due honor from a king. Alexander ordered his men to take up the corpse. Darius would be borne home at last, and buried among his ancestors with proper ceremony in the ruins of Persepolis.

If Alexander's troops believed that Darius's death must surely end their service, they labored under that illusion only briefly. To consolidate their grasp on the empire, their king declared, they must now hunt down and destroy the pretender Bessus. There was no time to be lost. ◉

CHAPTER FIVE

[AGE 26–32   YEAR 330–323 BC]

THE FALL

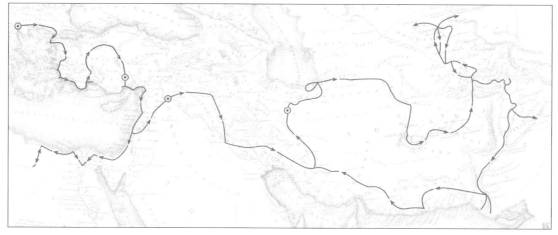

Above: A marble copy of a bronze bust dating from the early third century BC shows Alexander wearing a lion's head. The lion motif, common in his iconography, denotes the king's link with Heracles, the legendary founder of his line.

Above: A rugged path winds through the Hindu Kush in modern Pakistan. In Alexander's day, these gaps in the mountains were gateways to India.

Opposite: Alexander and his most formidable enemy, the Indian king Porus, meet on the battlefield in this eighteenth-century painting by Francesco Fontebasso.

FOR A TIME, THE HOMERIC GRANDEUR of pitched battles was over. Alexander was entering a new phase of warfare: grueling, nerve-shredding guerrilla fighting, often over uncharted and devastatingly harsh terrain. Macedonians would drop in the sands of scorching deserts or perish in mountain snows, where gaunt and hungry soldiers sometimes froze solid to the ground they lay on or the trees they leaned against. This adversity would call forth the finest in Alexander—and the murderous worst.

As the miles stretched on and on, his native suspicion edged toward paranoia and his pride toward megalomania. Many suffered for it, himself not the least. But still he pressed forward, gripped and set apart by some vision that he alone could see. There was a Greek word for it, *pothos*, a compulsion

to attain the unreachable, explore the unknowable. It was as though he wove with every step some glorious, invisible tapestry; and if it often unraveled behind him, its design nevertheless unfolded constantly ahead, stretching to the edge of his horizon, epic and grand.

With Darius gone, Alexander was soon in pursuit of the self-styled new Great King, Bessus, who was headed for his home province of Bactria. But Bessus's trail was cold, and the chase was soon suspended. Alexander marched north to Zadracarta, capital of Hyrcania, to ponder his next move.

Ironically, having harried Darius to his death, Alexander now became his late enemy's avenger—insofar, at least, as it suited his purposes. He marked Bessus for death as a regicide and usurper, but he was willing enough to forgive the other assassins when it seemed useful. There was, for instance, Nabarzanes, Darius's perfidious grand vizier. Promised safe passage by Alexander, who probably deemed it wise to separate him from Bessus, Nabarzanes scurried to Zadracarta with lavish gifts for his new lord. The most intriguing of these by far was a Persian youth named Bagoas, a boy whose beauty was so remarkable that he had been castrated in an effort to preserve it. The eunuch had been a favorite of Darius's, and now he took up the same function for Alexander. Their affair, while in no way altering the relationship between Alexander and Hephaestion, would last for the rest of Alexander's life and would exert considerable influence over the king. Bagoas found many ways to make himself useful, among them helping to lead his master through the labyrinth of Persian court protocol.

Of course this did not sit well with the Macedonians, particularly with the army's Old Guard, perplexed and irked at watching the king become more Persian by the day. Neither were the veterans pleased at the foreigners infiltrating their ranks, sometimes at the highest levels. Among the well-born Persians who came over to Alexander after the Great King's death were Darius's brother, Oxyathres, who joined the Companion Cavalry.

As grumbling among the Macedonians increased, Alexander applied the most reliable antidote: work. He marched his men eastward from Zadracarta into the satrapy of Areia, beginning a long, looping trek to the south to pacify Areia and Arachosia. It was frustrating work, marked by alliances that vanished as soon as Alexander turned his back and by native revolts that caused him to retrace his steps. Meanwhile, far to the north in Bactria, Bessus was steadily gaining

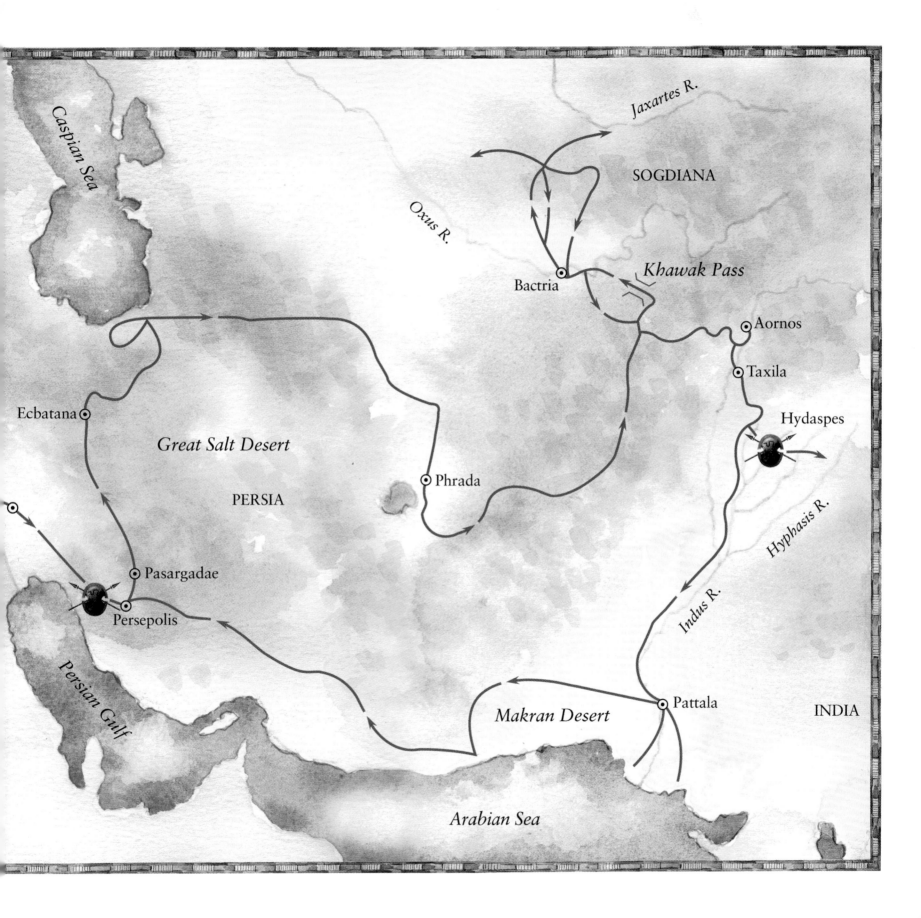

Caspian Sea

Jaxartes R.

SOGDIANA

Oxus R.

Khawak Pass

Bactria

Aornos

Taxila

Hydaspes

Ecbatana

Great Salt Desert

PERSIA

Phrada

Hyphasis R.

Pasargadae

Indus R.

Persepolis

Persian Gulf

Pattala

Makran Desert

INDIA

Arabian Sea

THE ORIENTALIZING OF ALEXANDER

Right: The formality of Persian life is reflected in this relief of royal guards, which was recovered from the palace of Darius the Great. The guards attending Alexander at his Persian court probably resembled these figures in dress and posture.

Having conquered the Persian Empire, Alexander faced the ongoing problem of how to merge two cultures that could hardly have been more fundamentally different—different in language, religion, dress, art, customs, and most decidedly different in the matter of the relationship between ruler and subjects. The rough-hewn Macedonians regarded Persians as decadent, effeminate, and slavish, and their monarchy as despotic. For their part, the formal and refined Persians must have deemed the Macedonians a horde of yokels and louts. Alexander's challenge was to remain Macedonian enough to hold the respect of his countrymen, while becoming Persian enough to command acceptance by his new subjects. It was a wide gulf to straddle, and he never quite satisfied either side.

Soon after Darius's death, Alexander began wearing a modified version of the Persian royal dress: a tunic of striped purple and white, a belt of woven gold, and a cloth diadem. He stopped short, however, of donning the tall, conical tiara reserved for the Great King, and the trousers and sleeved overcoat—customary royal attire that the Macedonians found particularly outlandish. The Persians probably regarded the new garb insufficiently regal, while the Macedonians viewed even the slightest concessions in dress as degenerate. Neither were they pleased when

Alexander began outfitting his Companion Cavalry in white and purple Persian cloaks and adorning their horses with elaborate Persian harnesses and saddles.

Worse yet were the ominous changes in court protocol. The Macedonians, accustomed to easy access to their king, were now faced with a gauntlet of Persian ushers and other functionaries who controlled all traffic toward the royal presence. The Persians thought it proper and respectful that their god-anointed monarch should be secluded and aloof. On the other hand, the Macedonians, barred by foreigners from their own king, felt rejected and enraged. Hephaestion and a few of Alexander's other close friends accepted the political logic of his concessions to Persian sensibilities, but they were a distinct minority.

By far the most objectionable of Alexander's proposed Oriental innovations was *proskynesis*, the Persian custom of prostrating oneself before the king. From the outset, Persians in Alexander's court greeted him in this manner. They regarded it as a suitable sign of deference; anything less was disrespectful from their point of view. But for the proud Macedonians, who went down on their bellies only before the gods, proskynesis seemed unspeakably servile and demeaning. Nevertheless, Alexander apparently intended to demand it of them, concerned that his status with the Persians was undermined when they saw his countrymen greet him while standing casually upright. Word might get around that he was lightly regarded by his own people, and on such seeming trifles the stability of his kingship might depend.

Aware of the issue's sensitivity, Alexander decided to try out proskynesis first among close friends at a dinner party. After dinner, a wine cup was passed from Alexander to his guests. In turn, each either drank or poured a small libation in the usual Macedonian way. Then, however, each guest was to make proskynesis to Alexander, thereafter approaching him to exchange a kiss of friendship. The kiss was meant to restore dignity to the guest and reconfirm his status as near and dear to the king. (Among Persians, kisses were exchanged between social equals or between the Great King and his close kin.)

The guests knew what was expected of them, and the ceremony went well enough until the cup passed to Callisthenes, Alexander's official historian and propagandist and a kinsman of Aristotle. Callisthenes was a man who could raise flattery to grotesque heights, and he had no problem hailing his king as the son of Zeus or sending dispatches back to Greece with wildly inflated accounts of Alexander's exploits. But he was also a Greek and a devout believer in the superiority of all things Greek. And one thing no self-respecting Greek should do, he felt, was get down on his hands and knees in front of another man like some Oriental lackey.

Busy chatting, Alexander failed to notice Callisthenes' failure to prostrate himself. But a royal bodyguard took note, and when the historian came forward for his kiss, Alexander was told of the omission and refused to kiss him. Callisthenes, an able enough academic but rather thickheaded politically, tried to toss the incident off with a light remark. "Very well," he said, "I leave the poorer by a kiss." He should have known better. Alexander let the matter go for the moment, but he would take revenge soon enough.

Still, Alexander apparently decided against demanding wholesale proskynesis from his Macedonians, perhaps reasoning that it would cause more dissension than it would pacify his Persian camp. Never, though, did he stop trying to homogenize his court—trying to create, in fact, a mixed Macedonian-Persian ruling class to serve his will. It remained a lifelong goal, one of the few that would always elude him. ▨

Above: Alexander leads his troops in this illustration from a fourteenth-century Armenian copy of the medieval *Romance of Alexander*.

Left: Alexander and Bucephalas conform to the aesthetic standards of the Persian Islamic period in this miniature.

strength as nationalist fervor coalesced around him. During this time the main body of Alexander's army (left behind after Gaugamela as he pursued Darius) caught up with him, and with winter coming on, the reunited forces halted for a time at the Arachosian capital of Drangiana. It would be a strange and troubled hiatus, with far-reaching consequences for both the army and the king.

◆　◆　◆

Three sons of Parmenio had started out with Alexander's army. Two had died in his service, and now there remained only Philotas. He and Alexander had known each other since childhood, but Philotas had never penetrated the king's inner circle. Alexander distrusted him and probably disliked him as well. Many did. Philotas was a pompous, abrasive braggart. Still, he was a superb officer, and this fact—along with Parmenio's clout—had landed him the most glittering post in the army: command of the Companion Cavalry.

One day in camp a young soldier came to Philotas with a third-hand story (he had heard it from his brother, who had heard it from his male lover) about a plot to kill Alexander. Philotas promised to tell the king at once. In fact, however, he said nothing. Perhaps he thought the story too far-fetched to bother with; on the other hand, he may have believed it and chosen to let the plot proceed. Parmenio's demotion had much diminished the family's power, which would surely rebound enormously with Alexander out of the way. Philotas's silence was ominous at best.

Undeterred, the informant took his story to one of the royal pages, and this time the tale quickly traveled to Alexander. The eventual upshot was the execution of several accused conspirators, along with Philotas himself. The evidence against him was weak. It was implausible, for example, that the informant would have revealed the conspiracy to a man who might have been part of it. Even so, Philotas was tried before the army according to Macedonian custom and condemned.

Before his execution, the doomed man was tortured. Alexander had ordered this with a specific end in mind: Philotas was not only to confess to treason, but to implicate his father as well. With Philotas dead, Parmenio could not be allowed to live. He would likely turn on Alexander, and he was well equipped to do it. Far away at Ecbatana, he controlled twenty-five thousand troops—nearly half the army—as well as Alexander's immense treasury.

In agony, Philotas confessed all that was required of him, and Alexander at once dispatched messengers on racing camels due west across the desert toward Ecbatana. They arrived well before any news of Philotas's death could reach his father. For Parmenio's second-in-command, the envoys bore the old general's death warrant. For Parmenio himself

Opposite: Ancient ruins crown a hill in what was once the Persian province of Arachosia. The site is in modern Afghanistan.

they brought two messages, a routine missive from Alexander and a forged letter bearing Philotas's seal. Parmenio was happily reading the second of these when his own officers fell on him with daggers.

Above: September snow blankets a road traversing the lower Hindu Kush on Pakistan's northwest frontier.

The assassination sent shock waves through the army, for Parmenio had been revered by his men. Only with doubt and reluctance did many swallow the story of the general's treason. But contemporary historians, toadying to Alexander, altered their chronicles accordingly. After his death, Parmenio was portrayed as incompetent and timid, a tether on Alexander's genius and daring. In fact, the old man had been a magnificent general who had spent his life in invaluable service to Philip and Philip's son.

As for Alexander, even if he believed Philotas was guilty (and this is certainly open to doubt), he almost surely knew that Parmenio was not. Even so, the Philotas affair had offered him the perfect chance to rid himself of the Old Guard's most venerable leader once and for all, and he was quick to seize it. Yet not without cost. Hereafter, the Macedonians who were still the heart of his army never quite trusted Alexander again, nor he them. Not soon, for instance, would he entrust his Companion Cavalry to any one man. With Philotas gone, he divided it between two officers he felt he still could rely on absolutely, his lover Hephaestion and his longtime friend and general Cleitus.

When news of Parmenio's death reached Macedon, old Antipater—perhaps getting nervous himself—summed up the matter well. "If Parmenio plotted against Alexander, who is to be trusted?" he said. "And if he did not, what is to be done?"

◆　◆　◆

There is no telling what prompted Alexander to resume his march in the dead of winter—perhaps the army's restlessness, or his own, or that of the hostile, barely subdued natives in Arachosia and Areia. Whatever the cause, he set out northeast on a long, slow march through rugged highlands leading to the Hindu Kush, the westward extension of the Himalayan Mountains. Bactria lay beyond. Trudging through snow and bitter cold, the army's suffering was terrible. Snow blindness and frostbite took their toll. Supplies were short, and hunger was chronic. So was exhaustion, as normally hardy soldiers gasped for breath in the thin air. Nevertheless, the army began its crossing of the Hindu Kush in early April 329 BC and made it over in only seventeen days.

For the crossing, Alexander chose the Khawak Pass, among the highest (at 11,600 feet) and most difficult of the seven gateways available. The reason was, as always, strategically sound. Bessus had expected the invaders to take the lowest pass. Surprised at their route and their fast approach, he fled north and west across the Oxus River from Bactria into the satrapy of Sogdiana.

In the Oxus Valley, the mountains to the south gave way to the plains and deserts of the central Asian steppes. By now it was summer, and the men who had so recently faced killing cold now faced killing heat. They marched by night, but even so, the stout ranks thinned as stragglers trailed behind or died. By the time they reached the Oxus, at least one important element of the army had finally had enough. The Thessalian cavalry—not coincidentally the men Parmenio had always led—refused to go any farther, and many of Philip's Macedonian veterans joined their mutiny. Alexander paid them off and left them to their four-thousand-mile march home.

Those who remained might have felt their own loyalty strained by their king's next move: Shorthanded, Alexander began recruiting tough, local tribesmen as auxiliary troops. No longer was the army a fairly homogeneous body of Macedonians and Greeks who had crossed the

Below: Alexander rides in a royal procession in this sixteenth-century Mogul painting.

Hellespont into Asia Minor. Now, steadily, it was conforming to the new shape that Alexander seemed to envision: a stateless tool of conquest that might roll on and on indefinitely, answerable to him alone. With his reconfigured troops, he pressed inexorably on, managing a difficult crossing of the Oxus, hot on Bessus's trail.

Bessus might have made a successful stand at the river, and his failure to do so turned out to be a fatal mistake. Just as he had betrayed Darius, so his own men—perhaps in search of a more aggressive leader—now betrayed him. Chief instigator of the coup was Bessus's Bactrian ally, an important noble named Spitamenes, who turned Bessus over to Alexander. Once in enemy hands, Bessus was humiliated and beaten, then sent to the Sogdian capital of Zariaspa to be tried as a regicide. He was convicted and, after Persian custom, his nose and ears lopped off. The pathetic wretch, once-proud aspirant to the Achaemenid crown, was then sent west to Ecbatana and publicly executed.

◆   ◆   ◆

Bessus's misfortune might first have seemed a windfall for Alexander; in fact, it was a curse. Spitamenes, who now took up the fight, was a master of guerrilla tactics, the toughest foe the king had faced since Memnon back in Asia Minor. Spitamenes and his horsemen mounted swift and savage attacks, then faded back into the steppe or the desert, territory as familiar to them as it was alien to the invaders. At one point the new general laid siege to the city of Maracanda (modern Samarkand), the empire's outermost northeast boundary. Underestimating his enemy, Alexander sent a force of only sixty cavalry and two thousand infantry to relieve the city. They were killed almost to a man. Badly shaken by the catastrophe, the king suppressed all news of it on pain of death. Eventually, he led a force to raise the siege himself and occupy Maracanda, but at little cost to the enemy. Spitamenes and his men merely vanished once more into the landscape.

The fighting went on and on, and Alexander himself was among its casualties. An enemy arrow badly splintered his leg, and later a large stone struck his face and neck, temporarily blurring his vision and leaving him hardly able to speak. Debilitated, he grew even weaker when polluted water caused a bout of severe diarrhea. Herculean though his constitution was, he desperately needed rest to recover properly, but this was a luxury he would never permit.

During the summer of 328 BC, with the army quartered in Maracanda, the king was on a ragged edge, physically and emotionally. Ever since Parmenio's murder, Alexander had been censoring his soldiers' outgoing mail—spying on his own men, in fact—and he was well aware of the unease infecting his ranks. The atmosphere among his courtiers was no better, with mistrust and dislike simmering between the Macedonians and Orientals. The war was

Above: A crossroads for conquerors, the ancient town of Samarkand, called Maracanda in Alexander's day, fell to the Macedonians and later to the Mongols under Genghis Khan.

Opposite: Alexander lies ailing in this illustration from a fifteenth-century French manuscript of the *Life of Alexander the Great*, a much earlier work by the Roman scholar Quintus Curtius.

Above: A silver decadrachma minted around 324 BC shows a standing figure wearing a Macedonian helmet, cloak, and armor and holding a thunderbolt. This is believed to be the only extant life portrait of Alexander. The medallion was issued to commemorate the conqueror's later victory over the Indian king Porus. The back of the medallion is shown on page 180.

going badly, abrading the nerves of warriors accustomed to victory. Maracanda was dusty and hot, and the men were drinking more than they should, Alexander among them. The drunken dinner parties he so enjoyed were frequent, in part because they sometimes helped cool resentments, but probably, too, because the king needed the release that alcohol afforded.

On one such occasion the courtiers gathered, perhaps to bid good-bye to Cleitus. The old general, who had been like an uncle to Alexander during the boy's childhood and who had saved his life at the Granicus, was leaving his co-command of the Companion Cavalry to take up his post as satrap of Bactria, a well-earned honor bestowed by the king. The banquet began festively enough, with the usual boasting and banter. But the men grew drunker, and gentle teasing gave way to outright insults, and the night descended into horror as long-nursed grudges and grievances finally detonated.

An argument broke out whose central theme—the most sensitive one possible—was the relative merits of Philip's achievements versus Alexander's. Alexander's flatterers were denigrating Philip, and Alexander himself was bragging more than usual and hinting that his generals were responsible for recent military setbacks. Furious, Cleitus rose drunkenly to declare that Philip's victories had been superior to Alexander's and that Alexander owed his own successes to Philip's veterans, Parmenio among them. Predictably, matters went from bad to worse, with Cleitus shouting at one point, "It is by the blood of the Macedonians, and these wounds of ours, that you have risen so high—disowning Philip, claiming Ammon as your father!"

"That's the way you talk about me the whole time, isn't it?" Alexander screamed back, warning that Cleitus would not get away with it. Cleitus countered that the dead Macedonians were the lucky ones, having never lived to see their countrymen "kowtowing to Persians before they could have an audience with their own king."

As the argument grew hotter, Alexander grabbed an apple, flung it at Cleitus, and began groping for his sword. The king's friends held him down while other guests dragged the general from the banquet hall. Unfortunately, he soon lurched back to declaim a line from Euripides: "Alas what evil government in Hellas!" Cleitus knew full well that Alexander was familiar with the rest of the passage from the popular play *Andromache*, which decried "self-important" men who "think they're above the people. Why, they're nothing!"

Purple with rage and drink, Alexander leaped from his couch and, seizing a spear from a guard, rushed at Cleitus, running him through and killing him.

Remorse and guilt now fell on the king like taloned Furies. With a cry he pulled the spear from his old friend's body and tried to turn it on himself before friends restrained him.

Above: Friends try to comfort a guilt-stricken Alexander as he grieves for the slain Cleitus in this nine-teenth-century drawing.

He then fled to his rooms and grieved through the night alone. In the morning he ordered Cleitus's body brought to him so he could mourn it.

Alexander stayed in seclusion for several days, refusing food and drink, before finally admitting his followers to help him rationalize his crime. It was fate, they said, or the will of an angry god, or justifiable in any case because Cleitus had been speaking treason. Most effective of the comforters was a Greek philosopher, Anaxarchus, who declared that the king was above the law, and anything he did was just. Alexander seemed to like that idea quite a lot. And if his Macedonians did not—if, in fact, they found the notion appalling—none was now apt to say so out loud. The murder of Cleitus had demonstrated emphatically that the days when a Macedonian could speak his mind before the king as a free man were over.

◆　◆　◆

Fortunately, Alexander's fortunes of war were improving. It had taken two years to wear Spitamenes down, but at last he was bottled up in the northern part of his territory, and a desperate

Opposite: Alexander weds
the beautiful Roxane in
this seventeenth-century
painting by Rene-Antoine
Houasse. One feature of the
wedding rite involved the
king's cutting a ceremonial
loaf of bread with his
sword.

effort to break out ended in bloody defeat. Afterward, many of his men changed sides, and the cunning general met a familiar fate: He was betrayed by his own allies, who killed him.

Now only an isolated handful of rebels held out against the king, but they were in Sogdiana's mountainous southeast, and winter was coming on again. Once more the Macedonians followed Alexander through terrible cold, and some two thousand of them died along the march. Ironically, this kind of hardship restored to the soldiers the general they loved: not the strange, aloof, and temperamental creature of the court, but the comrade who shared their pain and helped hold it at bay with the praise and encouragement that kept them moving forward when every step seemed impossible. He had trees felled for firewood all along the icy trek, and sometimes he personally went to the aid of men who were faltering, half dragging them onward, knowing that those who dropped would freeze where they fell. One night a soldier who had gotten lost in a forest staggered into camp nearly fainting, and Alexander led him to his own seat by the fire. As soon as the man realized where he was, he lurched to his feet again, but the king bade him stay put, joking gently that the soldier was lucky to serve a Macedonian and not a Persian: By Persian custom, sitting in the king's chair was a capital offense.

So on they went. The season's campaign proved successful. Pockets of resistance were subdued, and the mopping-up operation in Sogdiana was complete. For Alexander, this latest triumph yielded two treasures that were rare indeed: a reliable ally and a beautiful wife.

He acquired both early in the campaign of 327 BC at a place called the Sogdian Rock. This was the stronghold of the most important of the remaining rebels, the Bactrian baron Oxyartes, whose fortress stood atop a tall, sheer cliff, well manned and well provisioned. Before assaulting the Rock, Alexander offered pardon and safe conduct to any troops who cared to surrender. This brought general laughter from the enemy, who replied that unless his soldiers had wings, they were not particularly worried.

Alexander loved this sort of challenge. He assembled three hundred of the army's best mountaineers, and at nightfall they began the dangerous climb to the Rock's summit. One-tenth of the climbers were lost, but by dawn the rest were raising flags atop the cliff. Alexander then invited Oxyartes' troops to observe his winged soldiers. The rebels were so astonished that, although they outnumbered the climbers by about one hundred to one, they gave up at once. And, in territory that seemed to breed revolt, Oxyartes proved a lasting friend.

Oxyartes was also able to provide the best cement for a durable alliance, a marriageable young daughter. Her name was Roxane, and she was said to be one of the loveliest girls in all Asia. Habitually rather indifferent to women, Alexander was evidently smitten with her at first sight, and they were soon wed, ending his years of royal bachelorhood.

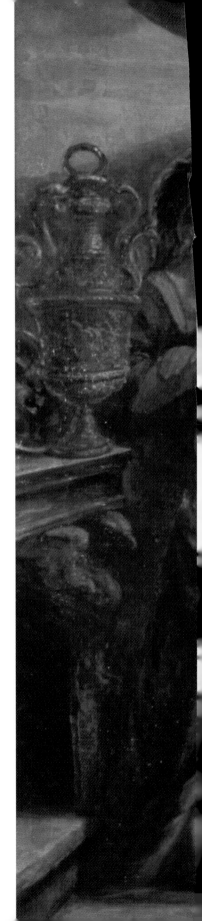

It was by most accounts a love match. Oxyartes may have been politically useful, but he was only a provincial chieftain, after all, and Alexander had his pick of Achaemenid princesses. Moreover, as a foreigner, Roxane was not a popular choice among the Macedonians. She and her bridegroom would spend very little time together, and it is hard to imagine what passed between them in their rare private moments, aside from sex, since neither spoke the other's language. Still, as women went, she was apparently the love of his life.

◆　◆　◆

Having subdued the great northeastern provinces of Bactria and Sogdiana, Alexander had now conquered the entire Persian Empire as it then existed. It was an astounding feat, setting him far ahead of any general of antiquity, real or mythic. Certainly it overshadowed the achievements of Philip, as well as the rather narrow exploits of Alexander's adored Achilles. But of course it was not enough. For some time, the king had been nursing plans to invade India. It was said that Cyrus the Great, founder of the Persian Empire, had won territory there that was later lost. Alexander meant to equal or exceed this accomplishment.

The Greeks believed the earth was surrounded by a great body of water called Ocean. They had no notion of the vast Asian land mass beyond India; Aristotle taught, and Alexander doubtless believed, that Ocean lay only a few miles beyond the Hindu Kush. He longed to see it.

Before setting out, however, he made more changes in his ever-evolving army. Attrition from battle, disease, and the manning of innumerable garrisons had left Alexander's forces depleted. There were only around fifteen thousand Macedonians remaining, though the army as a whole was much larger, swollen with continuing levies from both Europe and the conquered territories. To bolster his officers corps and ensure that he had a future army as effective as the Macedonians had been in the past, he now recruited thirty thousand well-born Persian youths to be trained in Macedonian warfare. Alexander called them his "Successors." By this he presumably meant successors to the Macedonian Old Guard, whose sensibilities, already raw, were now flayed anew.

Nevertheless, in the late spring of 327 BC the army followed him back across the Hindu Kush, this time via the twelve-thousand-foot-high Salang Pass, and made its way down into the Punjab. Soon the king divided his forces to begin the systematic conquest of the region. Troops under Hephaestion and a second veteran, Perdiccas, were dispatched east through the Khyber Pass. They were to proceed to the Indus River, subduing territory along the way and preparing the river for crossing. With the rest of the army, Alexander would campaign in the more northerly hill country.

Below: The tomb of Cyrus the Great, founder of the Persian Empire, still stands in southern Iran on the ancient site of Pasargadae near Persepolis. Cyrus had been the world's most renowned conqueror prior to Alexander's advent, and Alexander made a point of visiting his grave to do him homage.

Opposite: The Khyber Pass, Pakistan

The king's mission proved much the harder. Many of the walled towns and cities along his route offered determined resistance, and he was wounded again, this time by an arrow in the shoulder. The campaign was nevertheless a success, as always, but a triumph won with a brutality unusual even for Alexander. When the towns fell, their citizens were often slaughtered. The worst massacre was at Massaga. There he assured safe conduct to seven thousand mercenaries if they ceased opposing him, only to kill them all, along with their women and children, because they refused to fight for him against their fellow Indians. Such disgraceful behavior may have once been beneath him, but now—whether from pain or fatigue or stress, or the isolation and unchecked arrogance of his presumed godhood—some inner wellspring of benevolence was drying up. Any thwarting of his will, however slight and from whatever quarter, was enough to ignite hysterical rage that was apt to be quenched by blood.

Above: This terra-cotta figurine of a fighting elephant trampling a soldier comes from the Greek island of Lemnos and dates from the second century BC. Elephants may have terrified Alexander's soldiers, but they fascinated the king himself, who collected a large herd. Probably for this reason, the great beasts later became major status symbols for ambitious Roman generals. Julius Caesar even took one to Britain.

Whatever his methods, Alexander steadily gained ground in India. He had concluded an alliance with Taxila, a rich and important trading center, and now his target was a vast territory beyond the Hydaspes River, ruled by the king Porus. In the spring of 326 BC, Alexander rendezvoused with Hephaestion and Perdiccas at the Indus, where a pontoon bridge had been built and a number of boats collected. The army crossed and marched to Taxila, where the king sent a message ahead, requesting that Porus meet him at the Hydaspes to present himself as a vassal.

Porus replied that he would indeed be waiting at the river—with his army at his back. And a formidable army it was: upwards of four thousand cavalry and fifty thousand infantry, along with three hundred chariots and, worst of all, two hundred war elephants. The Macedonians had probably never seen these great beasts, but the animals were said to be fierce indeed. Without delay, Alexander marched to the southeast.

Left: An elephant and his mahout geared for battle adorn this Etruscan-style plate dating from the third century BC.

His timing was bad. By now it was June, the beginning of the monsoon season. Earth turned to red mud as the soldiers slogged through hot and unrelenting rain. Amazingly, they covered the ground in only two days, approaching what would be Alexander's last, great pitched battle, in some ways his most complex, difficult, and brilliant.

The rain-bloated Hydaspes now rushed at floodtide, and the most likely ford was where the stream narrowed. But here Porus waited, his army partly obscured behind a front of eighty-five elephants that faced the Macedonians across the roaring river. Crossing here was impossible, so Alexander commenced days of psychological warfare, by turns pretending to dig in and wait out the rains, or noisily feigning night attacks. Meanwhile, he scouted upstream to the northeast for another ford.

Above: Macedonian soldiers armed with sarissas face King Porus and his war elephant in this twentieth-century watercolor by Peter Connolly. In fact, the weapons that proved most effective against the elephants were spears and axes, wielded at perilously close range.

He found one about eighteen miles away, where the Hydaspes was bisected by a large, forested island, and there he sped with nearly sixteen thousand of his best troops. He left behind most of the army, under the command of his able general Craterus. This rear force continued to pretend to mount a crossing, a fiction enhanced by the presence of a soldier disguised as Alexander.

The fording upstream proved difficult but manageable, with men and horses starting out well before dawn on rafts and boats. Considering the weather conditions, the feat was executed with amazing speed. Porus soon heard of it, however, and sent one of his sons with a force of 120 chariots and 2,000 infantry to stop it. They were too late. Many Indians died in the ensuing skirmish, Porus's son among them. The Macedonians, formed up for battle with cavalry on the right, infantry on the left, and mounted archers out front, began moving downstream.

Porus now faced a difficult choice. If he moved against Alexander, Craterus could cross and attack his exposed rear. If he stood his ground, the two elements of the enemy army might trap him in a pincer movement. Wisely, he moved upstream to face Alexander, taking with him some 22,000 troops, including 2,000 horses, along with 180 chariots and 130 elephants. He stayed on sandy ground, keeping his chariots and elephants out of the mud. His front was elephants interspersed with infantry in a line stretching perhaps nearly three miles. Chariots, cavalry, and more infantry covered his flanks.

Alexander decided he must take on the cavalry first. Fortunately, the Indian riders were well away from the elephants; horses were terrified of the big beasts, which could render cavalry almost useless. To accomplish his aim, the king came up with his usual tactic of misdirection. Keeping two of his own cavalry divisions hidden behind high ground, he would attack Porus's right wing with a force slightly smaller than the enemy's, hoping to lure Porus into transferring all his cavalry to the right for a decisive kill.

After an arrow barrage that neutralized most of the chariots, Alexander and the companions charged. Porus, watching from atop his elephant, assessed the numbers and took the bait. When the entire Indian cavalry was committed, Alexander sprang the trap. His hidden horsemen, led by the general Coenus, galloped behind the enemy's rear. As the Indian army turned about to face the new threat, the phalanx moved in. Enemy foot soldiers were no problem for these Macedonian veterans, but the elephants, controlled by expert native mahouts, were another matter. Alexander's men shot the mahouts and hacked and speared the great beasts to some effect. Even so, the elephants were the most terrible fighting machines they had ever seen, able to crush a man to pulp with a single step, skewer him on their mighty tusks, or pick him up with their trunks and dash his brains out against the ground. The memory of them was indelible, and no soldier wanted to face them ever again.

Eventually, however, even these mammoths turned, moving into the Indian lines and causing almost as much havoc there as they had against the Macedonians. Now the phalanx locked shield to shield and moved in for the finish. The slaughter was terrible, the end certain. Those Indians who drifted to the southeast were finished off by Craterus, who had by now made his own crossing.

Porus was no Darius. The king fought to the finish, personally leading a last, desperate elephant charge. If he won nothing else that day, he won Alexander's respect. In the pouring rain, the two kings met at last on the battlefield. Porus had dismounted and, drenched and bloody though he was, he looked magnificent, uncommonly handsome and standing nearly seven and a half feet tall. Even on horseback, Alexander could scarcely meet him eye to eye. Alexander asked him how he wished to be treated.

"Like a king," Porus said simply.

Alexander replied that he would do that on his own account, but he wanted to know if there was anything else.

Below: The obverse of the commemorative decadrachma issued by Alexander after his victory at the Hydaspes shows the conqueror routing a war elephant, perhaps the one bearing King Porus and his mahout.

Opposite: A victorious Alexander greets his wounded foe Porus in this detail from a Charles Le Brun painting. Most likely, however, Porus was still on his feet when the meeting on the rain-soaked Hydaspes River battlefield took place.

THE PAGES' PLOT

Alexander's customary campaign entourage included his royal pages, some fifty well-born Macedonian youths in their midteens who helped guard the king and perform mundane personal tasks. While the Macedonian army was still in Bactria, five of these boys were implicated in an assassination plot against their master. Some of them were sons of men who had been demoted from high posts in Alexander's service, and one boy had a more personal grudge as well. During a hunting party, the youth had peremptorily speared a wild boar, violating the custom of giving the king first crack at the quarry. Alexander had ordered him thrashed for his impertinence.

Guarding the royal quarters at night was a rotating duty for the pages, and the conspirators plotted to wait until one of them drew the assignment, at which time he would stab the king to death while he slept. For once, however, Alexander benefited from drinking too much. The dinner party he attended on the crucial night stretched on and on, and by the time the king staggered home at daybreak, the guard shift had changed.

Before long, word of the plot leaked out, and the five conspirators were duly arrested, tortured, tried, and stoned to death. Their guilt was beyond doubt. During the trial, the ringleader, knowing that all was lost, even took the opportunity to denounce Alexander for despotism, drunkenness, pandering to the Persians, and other shortcomings. But what the conspirators did not do, even under torture, was implicate anyone else in the plot.

Undeterred by this fact, Alexander took advantage of what must have seemed a heaven-sent opportunity to avenge himself on Callisthenes, his Greek historian. Callisthenes' duties included tutoring the pages, and he was thus vulnerable to a charge of instigating the assassination attempt. The allegation was almost surely hollow, as the king knew. Callisthenes may have held forth at times on the virtues of democracy and vices of tyranny, but if he was guilty of anything, it was of being a tiresome windbag—and of crossing Alexander. When the academic sabotaged the king's experiment to compel proskynesis among the Macedonians, he sealed his own doom.

Accounts vary on his exact fate. According to some sources, he was tried and immediately thereafter hanged. Others say that, kept in a cage and much abused, he was carted along with the army until he eventually died of disease. ▨

"Everything is contained in that one request," said the king.

It was a request that Alexander honored, confirming Porus's kingship and in time putting additional territory under his control. The king, an honorable man who would prove a faithful ally, fared well in defeat.

In victory, however, Alexander suffered a woeful loss. Bucephalas, injured in the early skirmishing, soon died. The valiant old war horse, history's most famous, was buried with great honors, and tradition has it that Alexander founded a town on the battlefield and named it Bucephala in honor of his friend.

◆ ◆ ◆

Alexander gave his men a much-needed month's rest after the battle, but the atmosphere in camp was as gloomy as the ceaseless rain, with hardly a glimmer of the jubilation that had followed earlier victories. The most veteran of the soldiers had now marched thousands of miles to this sodden, hellish place, and they hardly knew where they were anymore, or whom they fought, or why, or when or if the marching and fighting would ever end.

Their king assured them that Ocean was near, and they would reach it soon, and it would bear them home. Few believed it. They knew that Alexander had, in fact, ordered construction of a large fleet, but it was not clear when or where it might be used. The soldiers had heard rumors of what lay to the east: not Ocean, but vast lands filled with warlike tribes—tribes with elephants. By now Alexander himself must have known something of the truth from local allies able to correct his geography, but he held the knowledge close. He was sure he could lure the men on as he always had, a day at a time, a river at a time, indefinitely.

In July 326 BC the army marched east again. Often there was fighting, and once a siege. Always there was rain. Rot ate into boots and sandals, fungus into flesh. Poisonous snakes slithered everywhere in the endless mud. The troops reached the Hyphasis River, where Alexander loosed them to pillage the countryside, certain the treat would lift their spirits. It did not. They were on flat land now, and they could see far to the east toward a horizon where no Ocean lay. And here the great and undefeated Macedonian juggernaut simply ground to a halt.

Nothing Alexander could do would budge the men another inch forward. He gathered them for an impassioned speech, exhorting them to greater glory. Once it would have been greeted with cheers. Now it

Below: This modern statue of Alexander astride Bucephalas stands in Thessaloníki, Greece. Man and horse had been companions for sixteen or seventeen years before the death of Bucephalas after the battle of Hydaspes.

thudded into a well of embarrassed silence. Finally, the old general Coenus rose to speak for the men. They were, he said, at the end of their rope, and they wanted only one thing: to see their homes again before it was too late. (Coenus himself would not make it; he would soon fall ill and die in India.) Alexander, he pointed out, could raise another army, but this one had gone as far as it could go. "Sir," he concluded, "if there is one thing above all others a successful man should know, it is when to stop." Now the cheers came, and they were thunderous.

Furious, Alexander dismissed the men and summoned his officers. He told them they could go home if they wished; personally, he planned to go forward. "And you may tell your people there," he said, "that you deserted your king in the midst of his enemies." With that, he retired to his tent to sulk.

He waited. If his words could not move them, surely his silence would. By the third day, though, he realized it was no use, and grimly he bowed to the inevitable. Now the soldiers thronged around him with cheers and blessings. He would never forgive them.

◆　◆　◆

The army marched back to the Hydaspes, where an impressive fleet of 1,800 vessels awaited. The plan was for a small part of the army to embark, while the rest, including the camp followers, traveled by land. They would proceed downriver to the Chenab and then the Indus, which would take them to the Arabian Sea—Ocean itself, as far as the troops knew. The fleet would travel west to the Persian Gulf, perhaps to the mouth of the Euphrates, there to eventually rendezvous with the land-bound contingent.

In November of 326 BC the seagoers—some eight thousand troops—took ship, while everyone else divided into two columns to travel downstream along the banks. The trip down the Hydaspes was uneventful, and the army's spirits lifted somewhat. But then native tribes began mounting savage resistance, and the Macedonians realized that another hard campaign lay between them and Ocean. Again mutiny threatened. Alexander managed to coax them on, but by now they were desperate, disinclined to fight, given to indiscriminate slaughter when forced to.

During a siege in the territory of the Malli tribe, the Macedonians hung back after Alexander had ordered them up scaling ladders. Outraged, he grabbed one himself, leaned it against a parapet, and scrambled up alone. At the top, he sliced through nearby defenders and, ignoring cries from his men to come back, leaped down on the other side of the wall. Galvanized by this fanatically brave and stupid gesture, his men rushed forward. Three managed to make it over the wall before the ladders gave way under too much weight. Inside, the three rescuers found Alexander, his back against a tree, holding off all comers. The three took the king's front and flanks and tried to protect him, but an arrow smashed deep into Alexander's chest.

Above: The Chenab River flows through the Himalayan foothills. Alexander sailed down the lower reaches of the Chenab to the Indus River on his hard-fought passage to the Arabian Sea.

Opposite: Alexander and his army cross the Indus in this illustration from the Quintus Curtius manuscript. The painting portrays conflict, but in fact the crossing was peaceful. The men trooped across a pontoon bridge that had been erected under Hephaestion's direction. It was a sturdy piece of engineering; remnants of the span survived until recent times.

He dropped to one knee, managing to stab one more attacker before fainting away. One of his protectors, his shieldbearer Peucestas, laid Alexander's shield over him and kept fighting. Then, in the nick of time, the Macedonians outside managed to break through a city gate. They flooded through, to be joined by a few comrades who had managed to scale the wall, and the king's body was borne away.

Rumors tore through the ranks that Alexander was dead, and they were not far from wrong: The wound was by far the worst he had ever suffered. The barbed arrow, six feet long, had lodged in his breastbone, very near his heart. He had lost copious amounts of blood, and more flowed when the missile was cut out. Either the initial wound or the operation punctured a lung, and a froth of blood and air bubbled through the jagged hole in his chest with every shallow breath.

For a week his life hung in the balance, and now his soldiers, however resentful before, were nearly hysterical with grief and fear, nurturing a superstitious belief that they could never get home without him. As soon as he was conscious, Alexander dictated a reassuring letter, but most thought it a forgery. Knowing that he must appear personally, the king had himself placed on a couch above a platform on a boat at the front of his flotilla. Watching from shore, most of the soldiers thought they were viewing a corpse. Weakly, he raised a hand, but he knew this was not enough. He ordered the boat pulled to shore and a horse brought. Summoning incredible will, he somehow rose, mounted it, and rode into camp, through deafening cheers and a rain of flowers. Only after he had dismounted and walked into his tent, out of sight of his men, did he collapse.

◆　◆　◆

The gods themselves could not have mounted a better piece of theater, for this one magnificent gesture restored for a time the golden aura of invincibility that had once surrounded Alexander. Fleet and army resumed their southward journey, subduing territory as they went, for now the men fought as though renewed. Toward the end of the summer of 325 BC, the assemblage reached the Arabian Sea.

By now, Alexander had divided his forces again, sending Craterus off on foot with many of the older veterans, three infantry battalions, and some two hundred elephants that the king had collected along the way. This contingent was to take a northerly route through the provinces of Carmania and Arachosia. It was a far safer passage than Alexander's impending march across the vast Makran Desert that bordered on the ocean. But the king was set on this course, probably because no one else had ever successfully traversed the Makran with an army. His plan involved coordination between land and sea forces: The army would dig

Above: Bordering the Arabian Sea, the Makran coast in southern Pakistan is as forbidding today as it was more than two millennia ago, when Macedonians died by the thousands on its scorching sands.

Opposite: A nineteenth-century engraving shows Alexander's surgeon tending the king's arrow wound after the Macedonians' battle with the Malli tribe. The artist captures the gravity of the situation, but the anatomy is wrong. The arrow hit the king in the chest, not the side, nearly killing him.

wells as it went to supply water for the ships, while the ships would carry a four-month supply of food for the army.

Most of the army and virtually all the noncombatants, perhaps eighty-five thousand people in all, would travel with Alexander. He was about to lead them into hell.

The journey began well enough, through fairly hospitable landscape that afforded both food and water. Then the troops encountered an unexpected mountain range that hugged the coast, forcing them inland, away from any possible rendezvous with the fleet. Food and water began to run dangerously low as they passed through arid scrub land floored with pebbles that in the midday sun burned hot enough to sear through the soles of boots and sandals. By now hundreds of men were dying of heatstroke and thirst.

Below: A marble torso from the Hellenistic period portrays Alexander as the forest demigod Pan.

Above: Inland from the sea, the sands and pebbles of the Makran Desert give way to parched and ashen hills.

One day the column came upon a gully that held a tiny pool of brackish water. A soldier rushed to scoop it up in his helmet and bring it to the king. All around him his parched and sun-blackened men looked on with an envy and longing that can only be imagined. It was then that Alexander had perhaps the finest, most authentically noble moment of his career: He thanked the soldier, laughed, stretched out his arm, and poured the water onto the ground.

In time the pebbles gave way to sand, a shifting sea of it that stretched as far as the eye could see. The land was literally poisonous, filled with snakes, the scant vegetation consisting mostly of toxic plants that killed the pack animals—what few remained. The men had begun to eat them, usually raw.

When there was water, there was far too much—rushing torrents that roared into the desert from heavy rainfall to the north. One night a spate slammed its way down a dry riverbed where some of the non-combatants had pitched camp. All the tents, the baggage train, and the surviving animals were washed away. Most of the women and children were killed.

Then came a sandstorm that left the column lost, wandering farther north until Alexander sensed what had happened and led a small contingent of cavalry southward. They reached the seashore and in its gravel sank wells that, at last, yielded fresh water. The army followed, and guides soon found a road leading north to the Gedrosian capital of Pura and safety.

The nightmare had lasted two months. Of the eighty-five thousand who had walked into the desert, all but twenty-five thousand had died there. For Alexander, who had hoped to grab a little more glory, the venture had proved an unparalleled catastrophe.

◆ ◆ ◆

Alexander's return to civilization was surely a relief, but it was hardly a happy occasion. Rumors abounded of treason and revolt. Some were probably true: Reports had spread that he had died in the Makran, and ambitious men had laid their plans accordingly. In any case, the king now sensed treachery, real or imagined, wherever he looked. The desert disaster had shaken him badly, and as usual when he felt his control threatened, he turned bloodthirsty. He began a wholesale purge of satraps and administrators, most of whom he had put into office himself. Ironically, two of the victims were officers who, on Alexander's orders, had helped assassinate Parmenio.

Moreover, to abort any possible effort to raise troops against him in the provinces, Alexander ordered all his satraps to dismiss their mercenaries immediately. This meant the coun-

Below: Alexander weds the Persian princess Stateira in a detail from the Alexander the Great fresco from Pompeii. The groom's cloak and spear distinguish him as the war god Ares, while the bride is dressed as Aphrodite, goddess of love and beauty.

tryside was soon swarming with unemployed and predatory soldiers, many of them exiled Greeks. The king would soon deal with this problem by blithely declaring that all were free to go home. Of course the decree caused political and administrative havoc back in Greece, where many of the returnees opposed governments that Alexander himself had kept in place. He cared little; Greece was merely another of his provinces now, and a distant one at that.

February of 324 BC found Alexander back in Susa, proceeding full steam with his stubborn effort to homogenize the two key elements of his empire. He decreed that upwards of one hundred of his top-ranking Macedonian officers would marry high-born Persian or Median women. He would lead the way by wedding two Achaemenid princesses: Stateira, a daughter of Darius, and Parysatis, a daughter of the previous Great King, Artaxerxes Ochus. Hephaestion, now officially Alexander's second in command, would also marry a daughter of Darius; Alexander looked forward to having his lover's children as his own nieces and nephews.

BROTHERHOOD OF MAN

Was Alexander a liberal idealist or a ruthless pragmatist?

Right: Alexander appears in relief on a gold medallion minted in the third century AD.

Over the years, some scholars have portrayed Alexander as a visionary who anticipated by more than two thousand years the political notions of universal brotherhood and ethnic equality. According to this theory, Alexander's Orientalization policy was aimed at creating a utopian kingdom in which Macedonians and Persians coexisted peacefully, unconcerned with ethnicity.

The theorists point particularly to the banquet following the Macedonian army's mutiny at Opis. This was a grand affair whose stated purpose was dual: reconciliation between Alexander and his Macedonians and between the Macedonians and Persians. At the feast, Alexander prayed for harmony and fellowship, but even the seating arrangement belied any notion of equality, or even integration: The Macedonians occupied one tier, nearest the king, with the Persians below them, and other races and nationalities below the Persians.

In fact, Alexander's motives were probably far more pragmatic than idealistic, and the banquet was just another stopgap measure to facilitate the full exploitation of two pools of manpower. He still needed the Macedonians. On the other hand, the Persian Empire offered far more in the way of men and resources for future armies, to be used for conquests that might stretch on indefinitely. For the moment, it suited his purposes to hold on to both and keep bickering to a minimum.

No sooner was the feasting over than the king pressed ahead with the unpopular demobilization plan that had caused the Opis mutiny in the first place. Interestingly, he ordered that the departing Macedonian men leave behind any Persian wives or concubines—along with their children, who numbered about ten thousand. The mixed-blood sons, free of any troublesome tug of ethnic loyalty, were to be given Macedonian military training—not exactly an innocent move on Alexander's part. And presumably, sons issuing from the mass marriages at Susa were destined for the same future.

The romantic theory of Alexander as egalitarian probably says more about the ideals of the theorists than of the protagonist, for one wonders how Alexander would even have encountered the concept. The aggressor's justification of bringing civilization to the benighted vanquished was common enough in his day, but this is a far cry from the equality and fraternity that were not propounded until the eighteenth-century Enlightenment. Alexander's tutor Aristotle had taught him to regard barbarians (Persians certainly included) as "plants and animals." For the king's own stated view of the matter, there is only his conversation with the priest of Zeus-Ammon at Siwah, as reported by the Greek historian Plutarch. The priest remarked that all men have a common father in Zeus-Ammon, whereupon Alexander observed that while this was true enough, god "made particularly his own the noblest and best of them." All might be brothers, in other words, but hardly equal. ▨

Above: A crowned Alexander and his new Persian wife mingle with other newly-weds while feasting at the mass marriages at Susa. The Flemish illustration is from a fourteenth-century manuscript of the *Romance of Alexander.*

The marriages took place in a single, grand ceremony in resplendent Persian style. But pageantry notwithstanding, the showy gesture was not popular—not with the bridegrooms (most repudiated their new wives as soon as possible) and certainly not with the Macedonian army, who regarded it as the act of an Oriental tyrant. Even less popular was the arrival in Susa of the thirty thousand Successors, the Persian boys who had been undergoing Macedonian military training. They were strong, able, bursting with youthful vitality and enthusiasm—and the very sight of them was an ongoing affront to Alexander's worn and long-suffering Macedonians.

By now, perhaps even Alexander realized that there was no way to heal such deep resentments, and he soon moved to rid himself of the worst of the dissenters. Shortly after the mass marriages, he traveled to Opis on the Euphrates to inspect an irrigation project. While there, he decreed that all his veterans too old or disabled for service would be sent home. Promises of big bonuses in no way sweetened the truth as the troops saw it: After hard years of faithful service, they were being cast aside. There was another mutiny, but this time the king successfully called the bluff, essentially telling the men that they could go if they wished; he no longer needed them. They soon came around, and there were tears of reconciliation and a grand banquet shared by Macedonians and Persians, with much talk of harmony and friendship.

Above: Wreathed in solar rays, Alexander appears as the sun god Helios on this terra-cotta medallion. The piece dates from the first century BC.

Opposite: Apparently comfortable in celestial company, Alexander sits between a god and a demigod in this stucco frieze. On the king's right, holding a trident, is the sea god Poseidon. On his left, grasping the head of his club, is Heracles.

In fact, however, Alexander had merely thrown a rickety bridge across a gulf that would never close. The feasting done, he continued with the planned demobilization, sending Craterus off to Macedon with the veterans. Craterus also had another mission: He was to replace Antipater as viceroy in Greece. Antipater was to round up fresh recruits and bring them to Babylon.

Shrewd old Antipater had probably seen the handwriting on the wall as soon as Parmenio perished. Now the truth was unmistakable. Antipater was popular in Macedon and supreme in Greece, too powerful by far for Alexander's liking. Besides, he was the last of Philip's Old Guard. Profoundly conservative, Antipater detested Alexander's Oriental policies, as the king surely knew.

The viceroy may also have wondered by now about Alexander's mental stability. The king had recently issued an edict saying that henceforth in Greece, he was to be worshiped as a god. Most Greeks found this laughable, but since it made little difference to them, they went along. ("If Alexander wants to be a god, let him," the king of Sparta said laconically. And in Athens, even Demosthenes remarked that Alexander could be the son of Zeus and of Poseidon, too, for all he cared.) But Antipater was sincerely shocked by the outlandish arrogance of this strange decree. Philip had never gone nearly so far.

Alexander was clearly not the same man who had left home a dozen years before, and Antipater meant to steer clear of him. A trip to Babylon would likely end, he knew, in a rigged trial and a quick execution. He stalled for time, sending his son Cassander off to assess the situation.

◆ ◆ ◆

Alexander, meanwhile, had traveled from Opis to the summer retreat of Ecbatana. It was July, and the lowland heat was oppressive. Given some leisure time, he staged a long and elaborate festival in honor of Dionysus. The king wore a celebratory face, but beneath it he was, as Antipater suspected, a changed man. Endless fighting, the humiliating mutiny at the Hyphasis, his terrible wound, the Makran ordeal—all had taken their toll. He was drinking far too much, and his erratic moods swung between extreme highs and lows. Now would come a blow from which there was no recovering.

One night after prolonged drinking, Hephaestion came down with a high fever. His doctor prescribed a spare diet, which Hephaestion followed only until he felt better. He then washed down a big meal with a half gallon of cold wine. Predictably, he relapsed. Alexander rushed to his side, but it was too late. His beloved, lifelong friend was dead.

Alexander's grief knew no bounds. All day and night he lay on the body, sobbing. He cut his hair in mourning, and even ordered the manes and tails of the royal horses docked. He sent to Siwah to ask if Hephaestion could be worshiped as a god. (No, the oracle said, a hero cult would have to do. Accordingly, Alexander ordered shrines to Hephaestion built in Egypt.) The corpse was embalmed and sent off to Babylon, where Alexander had commissioned an outlandish funeral pyre—a five-tiered, gilt-encrusted monstrosity with room inside for singers to chant dirges. It cost ten thousand talents, and an even greater sum was being spent for an appropriate tomb.

And as always, there was the balm of bloodshed. Hephaestion's doctor was crucified, and when winter came, Alexander annihilated a mountain tribe near Ecbatana—an offering, he said, "to the shade of Hephaestion."

If the grief never ended, it did in time subside. There was so much to attend to, including the myriad details of imperial administration. Such things bored the king, but there were also new plans that engaged his imagination and brought on spates of manic energy—plans for more exploration and conquest. Several targets were being considered, including Arabia and Carthage, or even Italy. He was laying the groundwork already, commissioning new and better ships for his fleet.

As spring approached and Alexander traveled to Babylon, the prospect of endless new victories lay ahead. He was still young, after all, not yet thirty-three, and whatever the tragedies of the past, he had survived them all. Nothing had ever stopped him. What possibly could?

◆ ◆ ◆

As portents had prefigured the birth of Alexander of Macedon, they now gathered to augur his death.

Seers warned him not to enter Babylon facing the setting sun, and for a time he superstitiously avoided doing so. But the swampland to the west of the city was all but uncrossable, and in time he did enter from the east. His first priority in Babylon was attending to Hephaestion's funeral. That done, he boated down the Euphrates to inspect drainage systems on the river's reedy, malarial lower reaches. As protection from the sun, he wore a broad-brimmed hat, its crown encircled by the blue and white royal Persian ribbon. Alexander was steering his boat when a gust of wind lifted the hat and bore it across the water, settling it in the reeds beside the tomb of some long-dead king. It was a bad omen, made worse when the soldier who rushed to retrieve the hat clapped it on his own head to avoid its getting wet. The royal ribbon was meant only for the king.

Below: The medieval *Romance of Alexander* shows the king seated on his Persian throne.

Not long after Alexander's return to Babylon, there was another strange occurrence. One day the king sat enthroned on his parade ground, seeing to the interspersing of Persian troops among his Macedonian infantry. When he left his seat for a moment, an escaped Babylonian prisoner—a madman, perhaps—wandered onto the royal dais, donned Alexander's cloak and diadem, and seated himself on the throne. Under torture, the man could only say that the gods had put the idea into his head. For a commoner to sit on the throne was, of course, a killing offense—except in one circumstance: When the stars foretold ill tidings for the king, another man might be placed on the throne to deflect ill fortune from the king and serve as scapegoat.

The days that followed were marked by a swirl of activity. Alexander spent almost every night drinking, as though to drown some inner unease. May 29 of 323 BC was just such a night, as the king hosted a banquet for his admiral Nearchus, with whom he was planning a voyage to Arabia. Uncharacteristically, Alexander wanted to go to bed afterward, but he was persuaded instead to attend another party. There, after drinking off a large beaker of wine, he suddenly screamed with pain and had to be carried to his bed.

He awoke the next day with a fever, but it was not enough to stop him from resuming his customary carousing that night. He probably believed that he could throw off the ailment, whatever it was, as he had in the past. But the small, wiry body, beset by so many wounds and now weakened by grief for Hephaestion, was at last beginning to fail.

By June 4, the fever, probably caused by typhus, was raging, and as Alexander had himself carried to his altar to perform his daily sacrifices, he may have sensed that death was close. The next day he gave orders for his officers to remain near the palace, and the following day he gave his royal ring to his general Perdiccas so that imperial business could still be transacted under his seal.

By now the king's soldiers had begun to gather at the palace and mill about, waiting for news. There were rumors that he was already gone. Soon his Macedonian veterans, long lines of them, were admitted to his bedroom to say farewell.

The night of June 9, friends stayed near his bed, and as midnight passed they pressed the question that now obsessed them all: To whom did he leave his empire? He could barely speak, but still he managed to answer.

"To the strongest," he whispered.

With that, Alexander the Great breathed his last. ◉

Above: A marble head of Alexander from the Roman imperial period

Below: A medieval, Christianized concept of Alexander's fate had him ascending bodily into heaven after his death. The ascension is depicted here on a twelfth-century AD cloisonné plate.

EPILOGUE

As Alexander surely knew when he uttered his final words, the man strong enough to be his heir did not exist. In his short career, the young king had conquered some two million square miles of land that in modern terms stretched from the Danube down through Greece, east to Turkey, south through Syria, Lebanon, Jordan, Israel, and Egypt, then east again across Iraq, Iran, Afghanistan, and into Pakistan. It was a vast and varied quilt of territory, basted loosely together by a single will. With that will extinguished, it began to rip apart at once. Sections would be salvaged and held by Alexander's Successors, as they came to be called, but only after nearly four decades of savage fighting.

In the immediate aftermath of Alexander's death, inevitable rumors of conspiracy swirled, alleging that he had been poisoned. The most popular suspects were Antipater and his family, but no case was ever made against them. The conspiracy theorists made much of the fact that both Alexander and his second-in-command, Hephaestion, had died only months apart and similarly: of high fevers following heavy drinking. This, they said, argued for poison. Contradicting that notion were the actions of Alexander himself. Had he believed his beloved Hephaestion had been murdered, he surely would have torn the world apart to find the culprit. But despite his rather paranoid turn of mind, the king did no such thing.

Opposite: A battle scene called *The Triumph of Alexander* is the theme of an Aubusson tapestry that follows a design by French artist Charles Le Brun.

Previous spread: The medieval rendering of Alexander's funeral cortege from the *Histoire du Grand Alexandre* shows the king's corpse in a cart far humbler than the actual vehicle. The real funeral chariot featured a golden coffin covered in purple embroidery beneath a gold and bejeweled vault some thirty-six feet high.

Neither, as far as anyone knows, did he say or do anything during his own lingering illness to hint that he suspected foul play. Also weighing against the poisoning theory is the opinion of most modern scholars that no toxin known to the ancients could have produced the symptoms that Alexander suffered.

Whatever the cause, Alexander's death left many of those closest to him vulnerable. His wife Roxane had been well along in pregnancy when he died, and she soon gave birth to a son, Alexander IV. Roxane then hastened to murder Alexander's first Persian wife, Stateira. It was a practical move, and one that Alexander himself would have understood perfectly: On the off chance that Stateira, too, was pregnant, Roxane was protecting her son's interests by eliminating a possible rival heir. On the fate of the second Persian wife, history is silent. Eventually, Roxane and her son moved to Macedon, where Roxane doubtless discovered in Olympias a kindred soul.

Alexander's mother was as fierce a protector of her grandson's inheritance as she had been of her son's. She saw to the assassination of Arrhidaeus, Alexander's half brother, lest he claim the throne. And when old Antipater finally died, Olympias, who had fought with him for years, continued the vendetta, targeting his son Cassander. She killed off as many members of his family as she could before Cassander wrested the upper hand and had her murdered. The manner of her execution is in dispute, but it is said that she faced death bravely, like the queen that she was. Cassander, who had loathed Alexander, also ordered the killing of Roxane and Alexander IV. The boy was in his early teens at the time. His death ended the direct line of Alexander the Great.

By this time, the late king had finally come to rest in Egypt. His body—expertly embalmed, perfumed, and gilded—had lain in Babylon for more than two years while a suitably magnificent funeral chariot was prepared, to be drawn by sixty-four bejeweled mules with bells tinkling on their bridles. This grand cortege was to bear Alexander home to Macedon to be buried among his ancestors at Aegae. But Ptolemy, Alexander's boyhood friend and always among his most trusted generals, had other plans. Ptolemy was claiming Egypt as his own, and, knowing the prestige attached to owning the royal corpse, he hijacked the funeral procession and took the body to Alexandria.

There, in the city he founded, Alexander lay in a splendid sarcophagus, whose golden cover was later replaced with glass or transparent crystal. Other conquerors would one day stand beside it to behold the young soldier-god, almost as beautiful in death as he had been in life. Julius Caesar would weep at the sight, knowing that in middle age he had achieved only a fraction of what Alexander had wrought in his youth. (The exact site of the tomb is unknown today. It was apparently destroyed, probably in the third century AD, during a time of rioting in the city.)

Caesar may have wept three hundred years after the fact, but at the time of Alexander's death, tears were relatively scarce. In Greece, for instance, where today he is revered as a national hero, there was great rejoicing at the passing of a man regarded as a tyrant and a foreign invader. Ironically, there was more grief among the conquered Persians, many of whom had deemed him a just king. Sometimes the profoundest sorrow was found in the most unlikely quarters: On hearing of the young king's death, Sisygambis, mother of Alexander's longtime enemy Darius, bade her family and friends good-bye, turned her face to the wall, and starved herself to death.

Mourning also ran deep in the Macedonian army. By turns Alexander had shamelessly manipulated his soldiers, used them, discarded them, or marched them through hell. But he had just as surely burnished them with his reflected glory and lent them a measure of his immortality. They had served under the greatest general of his time, arguably the greatest of all time. What other men could claim as much?

Whether mourned or reviled, Alexander had left a world much different from the one he had entered. His signal achievement was the destruction of the Persian Empire, since, with its collapse, there was no longer any impediment to the flow of Greek culture from the eastern rim of the Mediterranean to western Asia. As far east as Mesopotamia, Hellenism would remain the prevailing culture until the advent of Islam in the seventh century AD.

This fact had earthshaking implications. Among other things, it allowed the spread of Christianity from its birthplace in Judea throughout the Hellenized world. The new religion's growth medium was the Greek language, the one spoken and written by Christianity's chief disseminator, Saint Paul, a Hellenized Jew from Asia Minor. The New Testament is, after all, a Greek document.

This is not to say, of course, that Alexander planned the changes that followed in his wake, or that he could even have envisioned them. His career proclaimed his essential nature as that of a destroyer, not a creator; in fact, the capacity for destruction was his unique genius. Nevertheless, destruction plows the field for rebirth, and all that was worthwhile in the Hellenistic Age—a time of unparalleled intellectual growth and ferment—must rightly be traced back to him.

This was not his only legacy. Having accomplished so much and died so young, he set a standard for achievement that endures to this day. In the Western world, every conqueror that followed him, every individual of outsized ambition and drive, would study Alexander and measure himself against him.

His greatness, therefore, is beyond doubt. His goodness is another matter. Unearthing his true character from the overlay of time and the accretion of glamour that obscure him is nearly impossible, though generations of scholars have tried. Many have failed to navigate the pitfall of judging him by the moral standards prevalent in their time, not his.

He was a warrior, and he lived by a warrior's pagan virtues. Chief among them were strength and courage, and in these he cannot be faulted. He was also capable at times of great loyalty, generosity, chivalry, and charm. Equally, at least, he could be perfidious, devious, cruel, and murderous, willing to sacrifice anything or anyone on the altar of his unquenchable lust for personal glory. It must be remembered, however, that in his world such unattractive qualities were, if not survival traits, at least requisites for extraordinary accomplishment. It is estimated that, in his Asian campaign alone, Alexander was responsible for the deaths of some three-quarters of a million people and the enslavement of thousands more. In our time, the numbers are appalling; in his, they would merely have been impressive.

Alexander had been such a towering figure that he eclipsed the men around him, though many were very able in their own right. After the Wars of Succession finally played themselves out, three major Macedonian dynasties emerged, each lasting until conquered by the next great imperial power, Rome. The Antigonids held Macedon, parts of tribal lands to the north, and some areas in northern Greece. The Seleucids, founded by Alexander's general Seleucus, ruled in Asia Minor. The longest-lived and most successful by far of the Successor dynasties was the Ptolemies, who flourished in Egypt for almost three hundred years.

It was this line that produced, at the end, the one Macedonian ruler who came to rival Alexander's enduring fame—a monarch very like him, as brilliant as he had been, as ambitious, as determined to see East and West united under one rule. She carried the name of Alexander's sister, the seventh of her royal line to bear that name: Cleopatra.

Had Alexander's seers truly been able to show him the future, no doubt he would have been pleased with this Egyptian queen, whose death ended the Hellenistic Age that his birth had begun—a woman worthy of his legacy, one who lived and died, as he had, on a scale that could justly be called Homeric. ✸

SUGGESTED READING

Macedonian Background

Eugene N. Borza, *In the Shadow of Olympus: The Emergence of Macedon*,
Princeton University Press, 1990; paperback edition, 1992.
The most comprehensive, up-to-date account of the Macedonians through the reign of Philip II.

General Accounts of Alexander

Peter Green, *Alexander of Macedon, 356–323 BC: A Historical Biography*,
Penguin Books, 1974; paperback edition, University of California Press, 1992.
The most complete modern account, written by one of the greatest contemporary scholars of antiquity.

◆

A. B. Bosworth, *Conquest and Empire: The Reign of Alexander the Great*,
Cambridge University Press, paperback edition, 1988.
The work of arguably the most important scholar of Alexander in recent decades.

◆

Ulrich Wilcken, *Alexander the Great*, W. W. Norton & Co., paperback edition, 1966.
A reprint of a classic account of Alexander by a great German scholar. Even if it
is a bit out of date, it is a solid, reliable interpretation of Alexander's career.

Military Matters

J. F. C. Fuller, *The Generalship of Alexander the Great*, Da Capo Press, paperback edition, 1989.
Originally published in 1960, this classic account of Alexander's battles and sieges
is by the important British general and military historian.

◆

Nick Sekunda, *The Army of Alexander the Great*, 1984.
Nick Sekunda and John Warry, *Alexander the Great: His Armies and Campaigns, 334–323 BC*, 1998.
Both books are part of the Osprey military history series, which has two
paperback volumes on Alexander, both well illustrated with maps and diagrams.

◆

Donald W. Engels, *Alexander the Great and the Logistics of the Macedonian Army*,
University of California Press, paperback edition, 1980.
A unique and innovative study of one of the least understood aspects of Alexander's campaign—
the problems of transport and supply of the Macedonian army in an alien landscape.

INDEX

Illustrations indicated in italic

TEHABI BOOKS

DA CAPO PRESS
A Member of the Perseus Books Group

Tehabi Books developed, designed, and produced *Alexander: The Conqueror* and has conceived and produced many award-winning books that are recognized for their strong literary and visual content. Tehabi works with national and international publishers, corporations, institutions, and nonprofit groups to identify, develop, and implement comprehensive publishing programs. Tehabi Books is located in San Diego, California. www.tehabi.com

President and Publisher Chris Capen
Senior Vice President Sam Lewis
Vice President and Creative Director Karla Olson
Director, Corporate Publishing Chris Brimble
Senior Art Director Josie Delker
Production Artist Monika Stout
Editor Betsy Holt
Copy Editor Jacqueline Garrett
Proofreader Marco Pavia
Indexer Ken DellaPenta

First Edition
Printed through Mondadori Printing in Spain.
10 9 8 7 6 5 4 3 2 1

Library of Congress Cataloging-in-Publication Data

Foreman, Laura.
  Alexander, the conqueror / Laura Foreman.
    p. cm.
  ISBN 0-306-81293-2
  1. Alexander, the Great, 356–323 B.C. 2. Greece—History—Macedonian Expansion, 359–323 B.C. 3. Generals—Greece—Biography. 4. Greece—Kings and rulers—Biography. I. Title.

  DF234.F67 2003
  938'.07'092—dc22
  [B]

2003062573

First Da Capo Press edition 2004

For information, address:
Da Capo Press
Eleven Cambridge Center
Cambridge, MA 02142

Published by Da Capo Press
A Member of the Perseus Books Group
www.dacapopress.com

Da Capo Press books are available at special discounts for bulk purchases in the U.S. by corporations, institutions, and other organizations. For more information, please contact the Special Markets Department at the Perseus Books Group, 11 Cambridge Center, Cambridge, MA 02142, or call (800) 255-1514 or (617) 252-5298, or email j.mccrary@perseusbooks.com

PHOTO CREDITS

akg-images: 30a, 60b, 60c, 124c, 165b, 179
Alinari/Art Resource, NY: 96b, 157b
© Paul Almasy/CORBIS: 149, 151b
© Archivo Iconografico, S.A./CORBIS: 28b, 39a, 70-71, 128b
Art Archive: 172, 180
Art Archive/Acropolis Museum Athens/Dagli Orti: 62b
Art Archive/Archaeological Museum Isernia Italy/Dagli Orti: 133a, 133b
Art Archive/Archaeological Museum Istanbul/Dagli Orti: 6-7, 12, 95
Art Archive/Archaeological Museum Naples/Dagli Orti: 35a, 84a, 104-105, 189
Art Archive/Archaeological Museum Salonica/Dagli Orti: 16c, 28c, 28e, 49b, 58b, 58d, 59a, 59b,
Art Archive/Archaeological Museum Thasos/ Dagli Orti: 195a
Art Archive/Archaeological Museum Venice/ Dagli Orti: 81
Art Archive/Bibliothèque Municipale Reims/ Dagli Orti: 136-137, 170, 182c, 184-185a
Art Archive/Bodleian Library Oxford/ The Bodleian Library (Elliott 340 folio 32r): 130c
Art Archive/Bodleian Library Oxford/ The Bodleian Library c.1324 (Bodley 264 folio 78r): 138
Art Archive/Bodleian Library Oxford/ The Bodleian Library (Bodley 264 folio 172v): 191
Art Archive/Dagli Orti: 50, 73a, 86-87, 88a, 125a, 135, 153, 154b, 155a, 155b, 155c, 162b, 164b
Art Archive/Fitzwilliam Museum Cambridge/ Dagli Orti (A): 129
Art Archive/Kanellopoulos Museum Athens/ Dagli Orti: 27a
Art Archive/Mechitarista Congregation Venice/Dagli Orti (A): 165a, 194
Art Archive/Musée d'art et d'histoire Geneva/ Dagli Orti: 93
Art Archive/Musée des Beaux Arts Brussels/ Dagli Orti (A): 130b
Art Archive/Musée du Louvre Paris/Dagli Orti: 42c, 106-107a, 126b, 145b
Art Archive/Museo Capitolino Rome/Dagli Orti: 24b
Art Archive/Museo Civico Orvieto/Dagli Orti: 35b

Art Archive/Museo Nazionale Romano Rome/Dagli Orti: 94a
Art Archive/Museo Profano Gregoriano Vatican/Dagli Orti: 193
Art Archive/Pella Museum Greece/Dagli Orti: 2-3
Art Archive/Pella Museum Greece/Dagli Orti: 188b
Art Archive/Private Collection/Dagli Orti: 192
Art Archive/Tiroler Landesmuseum Innsbruck/Dagli Orti: 195b
Art Archive/Victoria & Albert Museum, London/Art Resource, NY: 39b
Art Archive/Villa Cordellina Lombardi Montecchio Maggiore/Dagli Orti: 150b
© Yann Arthus-Bertrand/CORBIS: 126-127a
© Bettmann/CORBIS: 43, 56a, 65b, 72b, 85, 106b, 148, 173, 186
Walter Bibikow/Getty Images: 183
© Jonathan Blair/CORBIS: 113
E. N. Borza: 21, 22-23, 44-45, 65a, 67, 69a, 78-79, 177
The Bridgeman Art Library/Getty Images: 17
Bridgeman-Giraudon/Art Resource, NY: 55a, 198
© Copyright The British Museum: 19b, 20a, 42a, 57a, 69b, 109, 110d, 111a, 111b, 122a, 139a, 142b
© Burstein Collections/CORBIS: 34b
© Christie's Images/CORBIS: 68b
© Lloyd Cluff/CORBIS: 187a
© Sheldan Collins/CORBIS: 31
© John Corbett; Ecoscene/CORBIS: 160c
© Corbis: 46a
© AFP/CORBIS: 203
© Premium Stock/CORBIS: 68d
© Royalty-Free/CORBIS: 123, 128a
© Ric Ergenbright/CORBIS: 168
© Arvind Garg/CORBIS: 188a
Getty Images: 142-143a
© Giraudon / Art Resource, NY: 161
Ny Carlsberg Glyptotek, Copenhagen: 24c
© Lindsay Hebberd/CORBIS: 184b
© Chris Heller/CORBIS: 90-91
© John Heseltine/CORBIS: 73b
© Historical Picture Archive/CORBIS: 118-119, 120-121, 131
© Dave G. Houser/CORBIS: 52-53
Courtesy of the J. Paul Getty Museum: 16b
© Wolfgang Kaehler/CORBIS: 19a
© Earl & Nazima Kowall/CORBIS: 171a

Brian Lemke: 49a
© Charles & Josette Lenars/CORBIS: 166-167
Erich Lessing/Art Resource, NY: 26-27, 40-41, 57b, 74-75, 76-77, 99a, 100, 101, 110c, 178a
Erich Lessing/Art Resource, NY Thebes Greece: 75b
Tom Lewis: 18, 63, 98, 132, 163
© Araldo de Luca/CORBIS: 37d, 77a, 125b
© Francis G. Mayer/CORBIS: 112
Museo Nacional Del Prado, Madrid: 45b
Archive/National Archaeological Museum Athens/Dagli Orti: 160b
Nimatallah/Art Resource, NY: 32-33
© Richard T. Nowitz/CORBIS: 89
© Diego Lezama Orezzoli/CORBIS: 80b
© Gianni Dagli Orti/CORBIS: 20b, 54, 178b
Private Collection: 11b, 28d, 37c, 48b, 58c, 64b, 68c, 75a, 80a, 92c, 110b, 124b, 150c, 154c, 164c, 182b, 190b, 212
© Carmen Redondo/CORBIS: 114a, 114b, 116-117
Réunion des Musées Nationaux/Art Resource, NY: 4-5, 29, 64c, 82, 83, 97, 108-109, 115, 140-141, 146-147, 174-175, 180-181
A.M. Rosati/Art Resource, NY: 61
Courtesy Saskia Ltd., © Dr. Ron Wiedenhoeft: 25
© Scal /Art Resource, NY: 10-11, 36, 38, 48d, 92b, 158-159
SEF/Art Resource, NY: 96c, 152, 156
© Leonardo de Selva/CORBIS: 88b
© Grant Smith/CORBIS: 134a
© David Turnley/CORBIS: 157a
© Gian Berto Vanni/CORBIS: 37b
© Rugero Vanni/CORBIS: 66, 144-145
Victoria and Albert Museum London/Eileen Tweedy: 169
Vilmar Collections: 80a
The Walters Art Museum. Baltimore: 30b, 190c
© K.M. Westermann/CORBIS: 102-103
© Nik Wheeler/CORBIS: 145a
Compliments of Stuart Wheeler, Department of Classical Studies, University of Richmond, Virginia: 46b
© Roger Wood/CORBIS: 51, 87, 151a, 176-177
© Adam Woolfitt/CORBIS: 72a